the COUNTRY BUS

John Hibbs

David and Charles

By the same author
The History of British Bus Services

A DAVID & CHARLES BOOK
David & Charles is a subsidiary of F+W (UK) Ltd.,
an F+W Publications Inc. company

First published in the UK in 1986
First paperback edition 2005

A catalogue record for this book is available from the British Library.

ISBN 0 7153 1939 6

Typeset by ABM Typographics Limited, Hull
Printed in Great Britain by Cromwell Press, Trowbridge, Wiltshire
for David & Charles
Brunel House   Newton Abbot   Devon

Visit our website at www.davidandcharles.co.uk

David & Charles books are available from all good bookshops; alternatively you can contact
our Orderline on (0) 1626 334555 or write to us at FREEPOST EX2 110, David & Charles Direct,
Newton Abbot, TQ12 4ZZ (no stamp required UK mainland).

Front cover *A preserved GS2 squeezes through a narrow lane in the Hertfordshire countryside
on route 386 from Hitchin to Buntingford on a Country Bus Running Day, 1 June 2003.*
Back cover *A preserved GS2 reaches the Surrey hill-top terminus of Boxhill (Greenacres) on
a Country Bus Running Day, 31 August 2003.*

Cover photographs courtesy of Ian Smith

Contents

The Illustrations Prints not otherwise acknowledged, and not from the author's collection or that of the publisher are: A. D. Broughall, 14 bottom, 36 bottom, 52, 85, 117, 124; P. F. Clark, 14 top, 45, 46, 50, 68, 76, 139 bottom; E. Course, 60, 109 top, 119; G. Coxon, 79; Demaus Transport Photographs, 35, 48 top, 65, 105; *Eastern Daily Press,* 147; J. Edser, 26; Charles F. Klapper Collection of the Omnibus Society, 24, 32, 48 bottom, 58, 82, 122, 123; *Lincolnshire Echo,* 39; A. Moyes, 10, 33, 38, 64 bottom, 77, 106 top, 139 top, 142, 143, 144, 148; F. D. Simpson, 12, 21 top and bottom, 22, 34, 36 top, 41, 47, 53, 57 top and bottom, 62, 63, 64 top, 57, 71, 72, 83, 88, 97, 104, 107, 109 bottom, 116, 127, 137; Richard Storey (Words & Machines Collection), 54, 103; P. R. White, 18, 19, 25, 110, 115. I am greatly indebted to Messrs Clark, Course, Moyes, Simpson and White for further contributing material which helped to compose the captions. Eric Axten has contributed the maps, as for so many of my books, and Jim Bray drew the cartoons and tailpieces; my gratitude to them for their help in making the book cannot readily be expressed.

Publisher's Foreword

The country bus has not been written about as much as the branch railway but in its heyday was loved just as much and improved the quality of life for millions of people in all parts of the British Isles. Only in its decay has it been less appreciated than the branch railway: it faded away from countless villages and hamlets with no special commemoration, no artefacts for transport enthusiasts to collect, no trackways to turn into footpaths, and precious few other physical remains.

To appreciate it we therefore need to turn to memories of those who ran it and to printed words and pictures. That the literature is much smaller than that of the country railway is also in part due to the bus's social role. On the whole it did not carry the young men with cameras touring new regions but more everyday folk, always a high proportion of women and children.

For them it was indeed a social service. Apart from the purpose of the journey, it allowed conversation. Reporting on the latest romance or visit to the doctor often began at the bus stop, and especially on busy early-morning journeys into town, and on market-day the noise of the engine and road was often drowned in a buzz of conversation—not possible on branch-line trains of compartment stock. The bus was seldom particularly comfortable but nearly always intimate. Certainly when I first made acquaintance with it in a major way—twelve miles to school from South Molton to Barnstaple and back each day often in wartime blackout—it was excruciatingly uncomfortable yet very intimate. It lacked the glamour even of the Great Western's undulating Barnstaple branch but was yet more part of the countryside through which it went, stops and delays caused by all kinds of things natural like ducks crossing the road and mushrooms to be picked.

In much of the British Isles it ran on a purely local basis without the support of people beginning and ending their journeys to other parts of the country or globe that even the most rural of branch trains carried. Often indeed it obstinately refused to connect with trains and sometimes was so local that strangers found it hard to discover its existence at all. Yet the best of the country bus services were those whose timetables had no regional, leave alone national, publicity — privately owned concerns serving perhaps a single valley with one, two or even five or six buses attached to a garage and taxi business.

When I undertook research for my *The Rural Transport Problem* at the end of the 1950s, I studied a number of such operations around the country, but especially in southern inland Northumberland. Their integration with the country was total. Drivers knew their regulars and according to the day of the week, time of year and the weather could accurately tell what kind of a load they would carry, whether a duplicate would be called for, and what delays could be expected. They would ask their wives to put lunch on the table at five to one or ten past two exactly.

Such services benefitted from local knowledge, from friendliness and above all from cheapness. Vehicles were kept running by improvisation and love and care, school bus drivers might be mechanics for the rest of the day, and empty mileage was avoided since the garage was usually at the end of the route furthest from the major town, the first journey taking people into work and the last bringing them home, or on Saturday back from the cinema. Small operators had many advantages over the larger territorial companies (mainly national chains) operating with new exclusive rights under the 1930 Road Traffic Act — and of course unionised. Yet everything possible seems to have been done to discourage them. The territorial companies prevented any flexibility in arrangements, for example the private operator often being unable to pick up fares over the last and busiest miles into town or forced to charge a higher fare. And legislation and taxation increased the burden. I witnessed it first hand; but John Hibbs, the author of this book, actually experienced it since in addition to being a keen observer from both the academic and enthusiast points of view he managed a country bus system himself.

Following the success of my own *The Country Railway,* it is perhaps natural that we should have thought of a companion bus book, lightly but accurately putting the whole subject in perspective, catching the excitement of pioneer days, the frustrations of later-day independents battling for existence against the territorial companies in part financed by the State — a book in which the very mechanical sounds, conversations and smells of the bus that linked country with market could be experienced. John Hibbs and I have had many communications about it. At least author and publisher care. I think it shows, and hope that many older readers will be able to relive colourful experiences and that younger ones will come closer to appreciating how important the bus was in the rural community. The countryside is the worse for its decline. Even the removal of the bus stop has robbed many settlements of a meeting point for gossip and a not-too-blatant hint to kindly motorists that you are intent on going somewhere!

David St John Thomas

1.   Introduction

It is half past two on a winter afternoon in 1956, in Cheltenham. Thursday is market-day, and the streets are full of people who have come from smaller places all over Gloucestershire and beyond for the shopping. There are lights in the big stores, and a cold wind in the streets as a traveller makes his way from the coach station in St Margaret's Road to the bus station in the town centre. This is not the Cheltenham of the tourist guides, but another aspect and function of the same town, serving a hinterland of villages and smaller towns for whose people the tourist attractions are largely irrelevant. For them this could be any of a thousand and more such market towns in the British Isles, where they go to find the larger shops and lower prices than they are used to at home.

But Cheltenham then was a unique example of transport co-ordination, famous for the coach station like the hub of a wheel whose spokes extended to London, Manchester and Bournemouth and to towns and villages throughout the South and West, and up the Welsh coast to the Mersey. For many a village or little country town the twice daily Associated Motorways coach was at least as important a link with the rest of the world as its nearest railway station, and while on summer Saturdays hundreds of duplicate coaches ran for the holidaymakers, the services always provided for more everyday needs as well.

On this January day our traveller has arrived at the coach station on the Black & White coach from Cambridge, and having left its warmth and comfort he is making for the final leg of his journey, the country bus that will take him to the Cotswold village of Bibury. The bus station, when he finds it, scarcely deserves such a title; under the street lights a couple of dozen buses are standing on an area of tarmac, about half of them double-deckers of the old-fashioned sort, with open rear platforms and separate cabs for their drivers. At the back there are one or two lighted offices and an establishment that is properly called a caff, where drivers and conductors mingle with passengers over their cups of tea. The elegance of the town seems a bit out of place in these workaday surroundings.

Most of the buses are best described as workaday, too. Painted an unimaginative all-over green or red, they have hard seats with low backs and are no different to the town buses that are passing on the street, taking their passengers home to the estates surrounding the town. Some of the town bus routes actually extend to villages beyond the urban limits, but for most of the country passengers the bus station is the start of their journey home.

The traveller walks past the row of green and red buses, sparing a critical eye for detail. Most of the destination blinds show the names of neighbouring towns, like Stroud, Evesham or Cirencester, but some display unfamiliar village names; few give more than a minimum amount of information for the stranger,

The morning departure. A Crosville Bristol LL6B waits on a summer morning in 1965 to set out for Colwyn Bay

but most of the passengers seem to know well enough which one to board. Here a uniformed driver is pulling himself up into his cab, while his conductor helps an old lady on with her parcels, his cash bag and ticket machine strapped over his shoulders, ready to ring the bus off. To the uninitiated these might seem to be 'inter-urban' buses, but most of the passengers will be leaving them before they reach their destination. They are country buses, it is true, but none of them is the one that our traveller is seeking.

At the end of the row the scene changes. Here there are five or six single-deckers that can reasonably be classed as coaches. Though they are very different from the underfloor-engined coach that the traveller arrived on, they form a marked contrast with the 'towny' buses he has passed by: they have brighter liveries and most of them have more comfortable seats. Some even have curtains at the windows, and whereas the green buses further back are just lettered BRISTOL, these carry the names of family businesses from places in the countryside around. The nearest thing to a driver's uniform to be seen is a sprinkling of peaked caps, and the conductors are busy putting parcels and pushchairs into the boot at the back of each vehicle.

Let us join the traveller as he identifies the bus he wants — it is still a bus, even if it *looks* more like a coach. The blind in the box above the windscreen of the driver's cab is faded and torn, but it seems to show the destination we want, which is a village beyond Bibury itself. Still, it's as well to make sure, so we ask the woman conductor, who confirms it, just a bit gruffly perhaps, but then she is off to the back with another pushchair. The sliding door at the front of the coach stands open, so we climb up two quite steep steps from the road, and find a seat. Our luggage — just a rucksack—is small enough to go on the rack above.

By half past three the driver has climbed the even steeper ascent into his cab, and the Gardner diesel engine roars into life. There is a familiar drumming sound from the unsymmetrical five-cylinder layout, but a comforting sense of power to cope with the Cotswold hills with our full load of thirty-five passengers. The seat is soft and high-backed, as we lean back and wait for the conductor to come round for the fares. This, then, is Harvey's Bus Service, of Chedworth.

When the conductor arrives we ask for a single to Bibury. Although most of the passengers have a return to give her, she knows the single fare and takes a ticket from the big rack. With a 'ping' from the Bell Punch at her waist — no new-fangled Setright ticket printers here — she hands it to us, duly punched, in return for modest payment, and goes on to the next seat. The few passengers who ask for singles will probably have come in with someone in a car, setting a dangerous precedent for the future of the country bus, yet who can blame them? Many of them obviously know each other, and several conversations have started even before we leave the bus station: one suspects that gossip plays an enjoyable part in them.

Women outnumber men by about two to one, and there are not many children, for it is still term time. A few tinies (who account for the pushchairs in the boot) settle down and sleep, and as we leave the streets of the town we become a parcel of humanity on the move, a microworld surrounded by darkening fields and leafless trees standing out against the last remaining light in the sky. So it has been for centuries, although for most of the time the pace has been slower, as the old carrier and his horse took the same road home. In the bus it is quicker, and more comfortable, but there is an unbroken continuity here, rooted in the mutual dependence — and mutual suspicion — of townspeople and country folk.

But that is over for the day, and we are going home. Up into the Cotswolds we climb, stopping only once, to pick up someone who has been spending the day with a relative, as to whose health and welfare a report is expected. Then we leave the A40 main road, and soon the bus stops to set people down, some at lonely corners, but most in the little villages that we pass through, their lighted windows a welcome change from the growing darkness of the road. We cross the Fosse Way and enter the lanes again, and by now the coach is hardly half full. Each stop has involved a round of farewells and a slow negotiation of the narrow aisle between the seats, not easy to do with a few shopping bags and perhaps a toddler in tow. Usually the conductor will have had to unlock the boot, and only when all the process is complete can she return to her place at the front, and set

The day is Tuesday, because that is market day at Saffron Walden. The market bus is waiting for driver and passengers to return before leaving for home

us on our way again with two sharp raps on the bulkhead window behind the driver.

At Bibury we too leave, with a word of thanks to the conductor and the knowledge that those remaining will have a subject for conversation now, about the stranger. But the door of the Swan welcomes us, and there is dinner and a warm fire and the deep silence of the night in the countryside to follow.

Next day is market-day at Cirencester, some eight miles away down the main road. The same towny buses we saw at Cheltenham run fairly regularly, according to the timetable in a case on the hotel wall, but we shall leave them alone this morning. There is a local family business that supplements their service, running two or three times each way on five days a week only, and serving the village of Barnsley on the way. (The day they don't go is Thursday, which is early closing day, and anyway it is the day people go to Cheltenham.)

We are outside the Swan at five to ten for the morning bus, but it is five minutes past before it comes round the corner; it starts at a small housing estate back up the road. It is a type familiar throughout Britain, with a coach body built on a Bedford chassis, and twenty-nine seats. The driver sits inside with us, for this has what is known as 'normal control'. It is not exactly luxurious, but it is clean and gives a comfortable ride. It too has a boot, but this morning there is little to put in it, apart from the occasional pushchair. It will be on the return journey that it will be needed.

We find a seat at the front, just inside the door. Mr Pritchett, the proprietor,

The coach is the place for a chat. This Wessex vehicle, seen at Bridgwater, is redolent of the 1950s, when the journey described in Chapter One was made

is driving, with his wife as conductor, and we obtain a return ticket, correctly punched. After we have picked up our last passengers there is time to talk, and we learn that they are thinking of disposing of their business — this they did, about a year later, to another small operator. Soon we are in Cirencester, with its urbane architecture and fine High Street. Once more the country has come to the town, by way of the country bus.

While the country railway has almost gone now, the country bus is still with us. Throughout Great Britain and Ireland journeys like these can still be made, in more modern vehicles it is true, but the people and the purpose of their journeys have not changed. Fares have risen of course: the big companies have put theirs up faster than inflation and have lost a lot of patronage, but the small businesses have often been able to hold back, having lower costs, and on the whole they have not lost as much. Even so many of them now receive subsidy payments from the county council. No one has sought to nationalise them, in fact the past twenty years have seen the state-owned bus companies withdraw from what they call 'deep rural' operation, and the number of small firms running country bus services has actually increased.

If proof were required of the dangers of overcharging, it can be found in cases where a private firm was first to develop a route, to be joined by a larger company. Of course in many such examples, the private firm later sold out, but where the two co-existed into the 1970s there were some interesting consequences. For the first, or 'established' operator was ruled to have the right to

At Fobbing, in the little-known marshland of south Essex, Campbells of Pitsea provided the bus service with vehicles like this Albion PH114 20-seater until Eastern National acquired them in 1956

An unorthodox – and anonymous – example of the country bus, this time in Pembrokeshire

14

make the later arrival charge the same fares, and in several cases this meant the state-owned bus companies being prevented from putting their fares up — and as a result, carrying more traffic than they could get on their other services at 'standard' rates. Sadly, there were other examples where the larger firm was able to force the other to increase fares beyond what was justified by the smaller firm's costs, so that traffic was lost by both parties, and eventually the frequency of the service was curtailed.

Like the railway, the bus has always been part of the social structure of the countryside. Its rapid growth after 1919 brought stable employment to men and women in small towns and villages where a carrier motorised his business or a returning soldier set up with his gratuity and his mechanical training. It reached its heyday in the ten years after World War II, before the spread of electricity (and with it the TV aerials) and the private car undermined many a prosperous business, but despite many unwarranted obituaries it remains a form of transport we cannot do without.

We shall see how its coming has contributed to the great changes in rural society that have come about in one man's lifetime. We shall share in the pleasures and problems of running country buses and the lives of those who work with them. We shall look at the buses themselves and their construction and use, and at the roads on which they run. On this voyage of discovery we shall visit little-known lands, for the country bus is a branch of the transport industry that gets on with its job out of the public eye. Let us look at it with a little nostalgia — and a lot of respect.

2. Roots and Origins

Even today there are people living in country villages who never go into the town. They do not feel deprived, either, but may even feel superior to those who keep gadding about. Fifty years ago, when S. L. Bensusan was writing his stories of Essex marshland folk, he painted a picture of a contented society, in which the 'sharrybang' from St Brigands-on-Sea (Southend) was an interloper, and the rare journey to the greater world started with Efrum the Carrier. A little poetic licence must be allowed to that, for the last of the horse-drawn carriers must have given up by the 1930s, when the network of motor bus services had become well established, though Mr Arthur Lainson once told the author that the last horse-bus in Suffolk ran from Wickhambrook to Newmarket up until 1932, when one of the proprietor's horses died.

Nevertheless Efrum and his predecessors had been jubbing along the Essex lanes for an uncalculable time before the country motor bus appeared, and so had their colleagues up and down the land. Long before the railways came, long before the stage-coaches that the railways replaced and before even the advent of the good roads, the country carrier had taken goods and passengers to market, and sometimes to start a new life farther afield. In 1763 the stage-coaches linked Cambridge with London, King's Lynn, Ipswich, Wisbech and Birmingham, and 'waggons' made similar trips for goods. The carriers came in from Huntingdon, Newmarket, St Ives, St Neots and Colchester, and returned the same day, save for the Colchester carrier who came on Friday and returned on Saturday morning, having a longer journey to make.

The carrier's cart was equivalent to the mixed train, with room for both passengers and goods. Though its origins are lost to us, it will hardly have changed much over the centuries, during which it played a part in the rural economy that is still played by the country motor bus today. Never patronised by the gentry, it was truly the people's carriage, and its extent and value can still be measured by studying the big county directories of the early years of this century.

These tell us that the carrier's business often started from some other activity, and must sometimes have stayed linked to it. Many carriers seem to have been millers, who would have had to travel to the local markets, while others were farmers, with a similar need. Household coal, which is still a significant fuel in country places away from the natural-gas mains, was distributed by small businesses, and some of these were carriers as well. It was a period that depended upon the horse for all short journeys, and anyone who kept horses commercially could easily enter the carrying trade.

The carrier's vehicle was generally a tilt cart, and while its prime function was taking goods, a bench could easily be put in for a few people to sit on. No doubt

Pride of the Marshes was the first serious attempt to run bus services in 'Bensusan country' – the remote Dengie Hundred, in Essex. This was as late as 1925/26

the more substantial growers had their own transport to take their commodities to the market town, but the surplus of the cottage garden would not be enough to justify that. You will still find examples of garden produce being sold in markets throughout the Westcountry by stallholders in just such a small way of business. People like that needed the carrier.

The trade was two-way. On the return journey the cart would be loaded with netting, rolls of linoleum, and a range of household needs, including stocks for the village shop. Much of this would have been bought by the carrier himself, on commission, so that his customers did not even need to ride with him. Indeed, there seems little evidence that in earlier times they did — Jackman's monumental *Development of Transportation in Modern England* has a good deal to tell us about the stage-coaches, but the carriers are treated as part of goods transport only. Perhaps we may reasonably assume that it was only the better off, who used the stage-coaches, who left evidence for later scholarship, and we know that those who could not afford to use the stage-coaches for the longer journeys made do in the stage-waggons. There is little doubt that the local carriers made room for them too.

Charles Dickens made us all familiar with the link between the stage-coach and the inn, and here too there was a parallel with the carriers, and one that was to last into the second half of our own century. From early times a carrier coming from the villages would 'put up' at an inn, where he could bait his horse, and

The country carriers motorised their services in the early 1920s – clearly with pride, as this example shows. The proprietor was Mr G. E. Jubb, of Upton, near Gainsborough, Lincs (Source: PRW collection, original supplied by H. Jubb)

the directories list the inns from which the carriers left each market town. The landlord would be paid a small fee, and would gain also from the custom of the passengers and — sometimes in good measure — that of the carrier himself.

The continuity was brought home to me some years ago, when I heard George Ewart Evans talking about the problem faced by a Norfolk abbot in the Middle Ages, when sending his carrier with goods for the Ipswich market. Although provided with cash to buy a night's lodging where required, the fellow preferred to spend it in some other way, and sleep under his cart. I don't suppose I was alone in facing the same problem when coaches had to lie over in London for a relief at nine o'clock in the morning — to prevent drivers from keeping their lodging allowance and sleeping on the back seat, we arranged for them to stay in a lodging house, and they were told to have the bill sent to us to meet. And I dare say the alternative use of the lodging money had not changed much in the intervening thousand years, either.

There can be no question but that the carriers form the oldest tradition that has contributed to the country bus, yet it would be a mistake to think of their 'motorisation'. Out of 310 carriers that can be identified as operating in East Anglia and Essex at the time of World War I, only thirty-nine can be found running motor buses in 1930. Of course there may have been others who sold their businesses, but there must have been a majority who gave up. This is not to deny their link with later days, though, because in 1930 there were 288 motor bus proprietors in the same area whose services were essentially of the same kind as the traditional carrier (including, of course, the thirty-nine already mentioned).

What is more, these country bus proprietors still in many cases 'put up' at inns in the market towns to which they ran. As late as 1955 the majority of the twenty rural operators running into Ipswich on market-day used inns like the Half Moon and Star in St Matthews Street as their terminal, even though their motor buses could no longer stand in the inn yard. And the landlord still took his fee, paid by the conductor 'out of the bag', but entered on the waybill for the guv'nor to see, while the driver and conductor each took a pint on arrival, and another before leaving for home in the afternoon — being market-day, licensing hours were unbroken on a Tuesday. In return the landlord provided a shed and employed a pensioner for the day, so that the passengers could instruct the shops to deliver their goods to so-and-so's bus at the Half Moon and Star; the pensioner then had them sorted out for the crews to load them into the boot.

The country bus as successor to the carrier is still to be found in many parts of Britain, and even the larger firms have carrier-type services in their timetables. The typical small operator would be based in a village in truly 'deep rural' territory, from which he might run perhaps to one nearby town on two or three days a week, perhaps to several. A mid-Norfolk operator might run to King's Lynn on Tuesday and Saturday, to Norwich on Wednesday and Saturday, and to Dere-

Here's another example of pride of achievement – and another Model 'T' Ford, this one owned by Mr W. Rook, of Laceby, Lincs (Source: PRW collection, original supplied by the Rook family)

ham on Friday. A couple of school contract services would provide the bread and butter, and, as we shall see, enable him to keep the market services running at surprisingly low fares, while his coaches would be free for occasional seaside excursions on Thursdays and Sundays in the summer, and the very similar private hire outing. All this, combined with a filling station and maybe a bit of repair work can still add up to quite a decent living for someone who takes an active part in running the business.

Another precursor of the country bus was the omnibus (the 'horse-bus' was an urban phenomenon). This one worked between Falmouth and Redruth, in Cornwall, probably succumbing to GWR motor bus competition in 1907

John Clemo's omnibus at Penzance, whence he ran to Truro. His brother Andrew ran to Camborne, and they were providing these services as early as 1879, serving the places that had no railway station

A Lacre omnibus of 1913, successor to the horse-drawn conveyances – this one looks a trifle draughty

When the railway came, the horse retreated. The stage-coaches could not compete with the trains, however much they cut their fares — which they did — because travellers found the railway so much better value for money. So the stage-coaches fell back to providing feeder services to the nearest railhead until, as the branch lines pushed out to serve every little town, there was no more justification for them.

At their height, the mail- and stage-coaches had combined to give Britain an inter-urban network of services that linked every place of any size, and provided access to the outside world for even the smallest villages, if they happened to lie on a coach road. (If they didn't, the carrier would take you to the nearest town, as we have seen.) With their decay their place was not entirely taken by the railway, and in any case the construction of branch lines continued throughout the nineteenth century and into the twentieth. Until a local station was opened there remained a need for access to the outside world, and to some quite substantial villages the promised railway never came. For their travel needs there appeared another alternative, in the form of the omnibus.

Eric Axten, whose study of transport history in and around the Essex town of

Halstead includes all the different modes, emphasises that it is incorrect to refer to a 'horse-bus' at this period, since the term only came into use to distinguish it from the motor bus. He gives the earliest omnibus in the area of his study as running in 1848 to Colchester on two or three days a week, and says it probably ceased to run when that section of the Colne Valley and Halstead Railway opened in 1860.

Before the Railway Age Halstead had been connected with London by a number of coaches working through from East Anglia, as well as a Halstead–London coach, while one worked from Colchester to Cambridge. The coming of the railway meant the end of these services, most of them having gone by 1848, and this broke the connections to Sudbury and Braintree, which involved long and roundabout journeys by train. While the local carriers continued, there would have been some demand for a better standard of transport, and by 1862 an omnibus was running between Halstead and Braintree, at first on market-day but later three days a week. (There is no firm evidence that it was the same one that had previously run to Colchester.) In subsequent years a number of firms ran on this route, which never had a railway, and eventually one of them ran also to Sudbury, for market-day there.

An advertisement for this firm tells us something of the country bus in its horse-drawn days:

S. HARRINGTON
18, Bois Field, North Street, HALSTEAD
RUNS

A LARGE OMNIBUS

FROM

HALSTEAD TO BRAINTREE
and back, four days each week
MONDAYS, WEDNESDAYS, SATURDAYS
and SUNDAYS

The 'Bus will start from The 'DOG', Halstead, on Mondays at 11.45am, returning from the 'ORANGE TREE' Inn, Braintree, at 4.30pm; Wednesdays at 11.45am, returning at 4.30pm; Saturdays at 1.45pm, returning at 4.30pm; Sundays at 6.30pm, returning at 8pm.

Parcels can be booked to and from Braintree daily, or will be called for on receipt of a post-card, or can be left at the 'Dog', North Street.

Parties driven out during the day or evening.

Moderate charges.   1st October 1915

Harrington's services survived into the post-war years, to be withdrawn in 1924 on the introduction of motor omnibuses by a different firm. The carriage of parcels continued the link with the carriers, but the vehicle had changed: now it was a passenger omnibus and not a goods vehicle with a few seats. Even so, the service it offered was pitifully slender compared with the frequency of trains on any country railway at the time, or with that of the motor bus that replaced it. But a hint of the future is the advertisement of its availability for 'outings'.

It was not unusual for omnibus operators to convert their services to petrol buses when these became available, either just before or just after World War I, thereby putting an end to the prospect of a branch line. One such is the firm of Norfolk Brothers, who still serve the road from Nayland to Colchester, as well as providing market-day services to other towns. The omnibus was more of a middle-class vehicle than the carrier's cart, and it was to become a significant factor in the days when motor services began to spread, and the country bus came into its own.

The extraordinary flowering of road transport after 1919, which had its origins in events well beyond the concerns of village life, was not unconnected with the railway. Two pre-grouping companies — the Great Western and the North

In a peaceful corner of the home counties, a Thorneycroft waits for passengers on a winter day

Eastern — were quick to see the possibilities of the motor bus for serving in place of a branch line where the growing capital cost of railway building caused them embarrassment when faced with local requests for service. There used to be some dispute as to which of the two companies was the pioneer, which can be settled by dividing the honours: the GWR was first, when it opened a motor bus service from Helston to the Lizard on 17 August 1903 (two of its five Milnes-Daimler vehicles having previously seen service feeding the Lynton & Barnstaple narrow-gauge railway). But the GWR suspended the service for six months from October 1904, while the NER motor buses that had started to run from Beverley to Beeford on 7 September 1903 continued without a break.

A number of railway companies tried their hands at running buses, but the GWR was the only one to develop into a bus operator in its own right, providing a network of services in certain parts of its territory that went far beyond the provision of feeder services to its stations. This was a product of the extraordinary period that John Birch christened 'the Roaring Twenties', when Britain came to be served by public transport on an unprecedented scale, in the course of which the country bus came into its own.

Not all of the pioneers were small firms – Progressive was 'colonising' Lincolnshire from 1920, when this picture of a Straker Squire was taken (Source: PRW collection/Phillip Battersby collection)

Still more substantial was East Surrey, an associate of the mighty London General, itself responsible for the NS doing duty here on a rural service, probably in the late 1920s

Although there had been a number of pioneer operators in the years before 1914, the outbreak of World War I still saw the motor bus as a rarity. Yet events in London had already cast their shadow, when the two inter-war giants of the industry, Thomas Tilling and British Electric Traction, signed agreements that restricted their further growth in the metropolis. By 1916 their provincial developments had met in south-east England, and produced the system of 'area agreements' by which their jointly owned subsidiaries divided the country up into a series of company territories, with here and there an area allocated to a sufficiently powerful independent firm.

Within its area each company could develop as it pleased, and since there was only a sketchy system of control by local authorities, the expansion of the industry was phenomenal. But while most of the territorial companies 'anchored' their routes to a town at either end — A. D. Mackenzie of the Southdown company in Sussex had a hatred of 'thin ends', and a firm belief in regular timings — they were all of them something more than inter-urban operators, for much of the traffic they carried originated from the villages along the roads they served. Charles Klapper, in *The Golden Age of Buses,* makes the point that Mackenzie and his associates laid a firmer foundation than did companies like National, which tended to stick rather to the market services of the older tradition, but all of them were engaged in expanding the opportunities for travel of the country people.

26

National, however—the National Omnibus & Transport Company, which had earlier operated Clarkson steam buses in London — went about the development of provincial services as if possessed by a colonising mission. In Essex, Northamptonshire, Bedfordshire, and throughout the Westcountry, they developed their operations by sending a team of men and machines to a market town, whose responsibility was to find premises, obtain licences, recruit staff and get established. Crawley, MacGregor & Simpson, in their study of the company, *The Years Between,* give this description of events in Bridgwater in 1920, where a service linking the town with Burnham in one direction and Taunton in the other had been started on Wednesday, 21 July:

> At first the buses were housed in a disused cycle factory situated in Carver's Lane, which now belonged to the Bridgwater Motor Garage Company. There was no office as such, and for the time being all clerical work was performed in the spare bus. A little later a room was secured in the Steam Packet Inn, which fulfilled the office requirements until a more permanent place could be found.

A service such as this, while ranking as 'inter-urban', existed chiefly for the benefit of the villages along the main road, for the GWR offered better connections between the three towns concerned. There is evidence here that the National had in fact learned from Mackenzie's dictum, that a service should be 'anchored' to a town at both ends of its route, with no thin ends.

A different approach can be found in the case of the Eastern Counties Road Car Company, which was founded when a group of Ipswich businessmen in 1919 felt the need for bus services to bring people in from the surrounding area. Instead of risking their own capital unaided in such an uncertain venture as bus operation still was, they approached Thomas Tilling Ltd, who sent some vehicles down, and quickly established a series of routes like the spokes of a wheel (one of them being the GER bus service to Shotley, which the new company acquired as a going concern). So as to save mileage, much of it likely to be almost empty, the ECRC policy was to obtain premises and establish outstations at the further end of each route, while at Ipswich their garage next to the Blue Coat Boy (approached by the delightfully misnamed Silent Street) later evolved into a sort of bus station.

Within ten years the whole of England and Wales and most of Scotland had been covered by a network of bus services, and there was scarcely a village that did not have a motor bus at least once a week into the nearest town. Those fortunate enough (or maybe not) to lie on an inter-urban route might have a bus every half an hour, which was a better service than the country railway had been able to give, and had the extra advantage of saving people the trip to the station. The big companies were not alone in this expansion; as already seen, some of the carriers and many of the omnibus operators bought motor buses, while

Successor to the carrier's cart, the fleet name seems appropriate to the owners' pride of possession

many ex-servicemen used their gratuities to set up in the business. We shall look at their motivation in chapter four, and in chapter five we shall describe the sort of buses that they ran.

What is most remarkable is the change they made in rural life. For centuries the pattern had been set by the market towns which served as the social and trading centres for a group of villages apiece, and while the catchment area of some of these was extremely large, there were many smaller centres within them, and the general distribution of market towns was based upon the length of the round trip from the furthest village, many such trips still being made on foot. The immediate effect of the motor bus was to extinguish the lowest level of markets, as the larger and better placed became more accessible. It took time, but in many cases they had gone by the mid thirties, while World War II put paid to a good many more.

With the closure of markets went the trade they brought to the villages concerned, but this was not the end of the story. In many ways they brought about the end of an era, completing a process begun by the railway, as the countryside became yet more dependent upon the towns. As late as 1958 there was one village in Suffolk (perhaps not more) where you could find a tailor — a man who actually made clothes — but he was old and on the point of retirement. Significantly, the village had never had a railway.

Other factors have played their part in the radical change in rural society, especially in the field of food merchandising, but few of them could have been possible without the changes in transport that have taken place with increasing speed over the past 150 years. What was begun by the railway was developed by the bus and has been carried forward again by the private car, with delivery vans and the nationwide distribution of goods playing a parallel part. In its contribution to change, though, the country bus has remained a part of rural society, rooted in the communities it serves.

To illustrate this, we cannot do better than turn to the north of England, where Laycock's bus service continued to provide just such a contribution to rural life right up to 11 August 1972, when it was sold to another long-established local firm, Pennine Motor Services of Gargrave.

Back in the 1880s, Ezra Laycock was the village postman at Cowling, in South

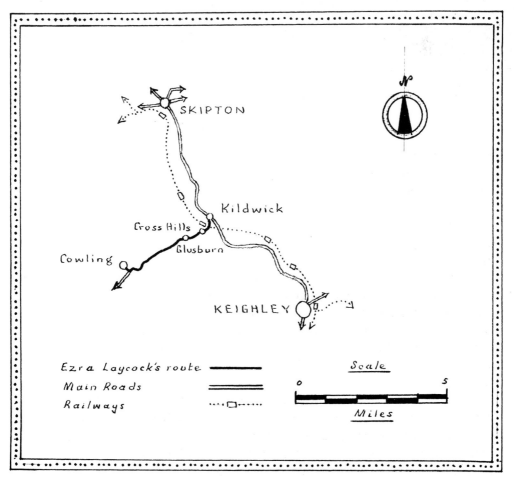

Craven, carrying the mail on foot between his home village and the post office at Cross Hills, three miles away. His father-in-law was the village coal merchant, with horse-drawn carts that fetched coal from Kildwick station, and other merchandise as well. In 1890 Ezra acquired this business, and five years later he was parcels agent at Cowling for the Midland Railway, and was also running waggonettes for passengers.

Meeting with competition from other carriers, Ezra decided to find out about the motor buses that, by 1905, were rumoured to be running in the south. He also went into partnership with a man who was 'mechanically minded'. Then he and his fifteen-year-old son went to London, and spent three fruitless days looking for a motor bus, without success. They heard, though, that there were motor buses in Brighton, so they took a half-day excursion by train, and sought them there — seeing one only for a few minutes before they had to catch their train back. This was enough, though, and Laycock & Stephenson proceeded to order a single-deck 30hp omnibus from the firm of Milnes-Daimler.

In due course the machine was ready, and a party of eighteen people from Yorkshire went to London to fetch it home. Three days later, after registering their bus at Bradford, they brought it back to Cowling in triumph, with the entire population of the village there to see. The 'Monster' was a success — partly no doubt because Ezra had specified a more powerful engine than the 20hp that Milnes-Daimler provided as standard — and two other local firms introduced motors in the following year. But the Laycock business survived and expanded, to become part of the dalesman's world — the fare to Cross Hills was 3d down and 4d coming back up, which accounts for the local saying that the distance from Cross Hills to Cowling is 'four miles there and three miles back'.

3   The Country Road

When the day of the motor coach dawned, one of the slogans of the touring firms was 'The beauty of Britain lies along her Roads.' Now that road transport has almost replaced the railway as the medium of communication and trade, there is little opportunity to go and see the countryside in that leisurely kind of way that goes back to the excursionists of Wordsworth's day, and the discovery of 'romantic landscape'. What is more, the dawdling coach is now just a nuisance as people seek to use the roads to get about their business. But the roads are older than tourism, and before the Railway Age they too were for generations the foundation of our society.

Another phrase that can be counted upon to stir the emotions of the Englishman is 'The King's Highway'. The 1920s saw that legal concept extended into another marketing slogan — 'The freedom of the roads'. Yet behind the verbiage there is a story that provides a continuing thread throughout history: the importance of the road as the means of linking communities and knitting our society together. In this the great highways have played their part, since long before the Romans came to Rye — Chesterton's 'Rolling English Road' has the ring of truth in it. But the country bus has little to do with the highways, and it survives on roads that have changed little in their alignment since the common lands began to be enclosed in the sixteenth century. They have probably changed less in their function than we might expect, as well, for the need to link the village with the town is as old as urban settlement itself.

For those who reckon ideas more important than things, the King's Highway is of notable interest. Far from being an elongated piece of real estate (which is what railways are), it is a right of passage. The importance of this right to 'pass and repass' on the highway has long been recognised. What limited its use was the lack of a suitable technology, either to produce a wearable surface, or to provide a vehicle capable of moving substantial quantities — first of goods, and then of people — at reasonable speed. So limited was the function of roads until the present century that the countryside and its people had changed little, and that slowly, for the previous thousand years and more.

When improved technology arrived, historical accident provided for it to take the form of specialised 'ways' — first the canal and then the railway. Even then, their principal contribution lay in the improvement of distribution, for the roads had not prevented near-famine from affecting some villages, while there was a surplus of food not many miles away. (This is a story that will be familiar to many administrators in Africa in colonial times.) Some of the late canals were built partly to improve 'social control' in the countryside, where food riots had not been unknown.

The new 'ways' replaced the system of turnpike roads, which largely fell into

Headlight masks show that this is a wartime picture. The life of the town seems far away

decay. It must not be forgotten that they were built by very capable civil engineers, and represented an advanced technology for their day, but the romantic notion kept alive today by a myriad of calendars and Christmas cards omits the dust that hung over them when the weather was dry, and the mud that they turned into when it was wet. Even when they were built and surfaced to the highest standards of Telford and Macadam they could not carry the heavy loads or permit the speeds that the steam railway allowed. And — for the most part — they passed the villages by.

For the turnpike system, with its attendant industry of horse-drawn transport, was essentially designed for inter-urban traffic. The toll-gates were resented by local people, though the purpose of the turnpike trust was to make roads passable where the resources of the parish were insufficient. Mr Pickwick and his friends journeyed to the Great White Horse at Ipswich; at most, they went to stay with the gentry at Dingley Dell; through it all, they remained townspeople. Above all we have in Mr Tony Weller the picture of a coachman for whom the countryside would have been as alien as it would for his son, Sam. By far the greater number of passengers that patronised the stage-coaches must have been drawn from the better-off in society, and a large proportion would have been travelling from one town or city to another.

Here and there a stage-coach would stop at the roadside for a few of its passengers to join or alight. Perhaps there would be a young lad leaving home to find work in the city, or to join a ship; perhaps more often the party would be like the one at the start of *Tom Brown's Schooldays*. For these travellers, whatever their class in society, the journey was exceptional — Jane Austen makes it plain that people who went to visit others expected to stay for some while. Yet the country roads carried another, more local, but much more regular traffic, much of it on foot.

There survives from those days a remarkable network of country roads and lanes. They emerge from the mists of the Dark Ages, some of them following Roman alignments, some of them even older routes, such as the Icknield Way. Looking into the remote past we can see the traders with salt from the coast meeting those with flint implements from industrial centres such as Grimes Graves in Norfolk. The local roads that linked one manor with another had their beginnings in custom and practice, and turned frequently at right angles to weave their way round the headlands of the open fields. Crossing the waste their tracks would be less well defined, and where there was rough or hilly country the 'highway' might extend over what today is one large field, with the waggons deserting one track as it became a sink of mud only to find another that would become impassable in due course. Often at the entrances to a village the road would make a double right-angle turn, making the village street easier to defend

The end of the road. Two years after this picture of a Crosville Bristol MW6G was taken at Rhydescyn, in 1964, the Welshpool–Burgedin–Oswestry service was abandoned

— a pattern that is often recognisable today.

But there were other roads too. Still to be traced in the form of long bridle-paths or hollow lanes, where modern agriculture has not wiped out the legacy of the past, there are the drove roads, over which the cattle moved to supply the cities with meat. Only the drovers knew these ancient tracks; men whose secretive existence may even go back to the Celtic tribes of Britain. The settled villagers nursed an ancient fear of 'the lad in the lane' — the 'green man' with unnatural powers — a fear that may perhaps be echoed in our attitude to the travelling people of today.

It was this ancient world of country roads — a term that still holds its magic in Country and Western music, and that was also a characteristic of the American colonies — that was to be changed by a process that began in 1663, when the turnpikes were legalised by parliament, and that has not yet come to an end. This is the process of road improvement, intended to be sure for the inter-urban traffic, that has also made possible the development of the country bus. It is this that has, belatedly, put an end to the isolated village world and broken down the barriers between the towns and the countryside, even more effectively than did the coming of the country railway.

At the end of the nineteenth century the roads were used predominantly for local movement — though the Post Office early in the present century transferred the parcel post from rail to horse-drawn road transport, between London and Norwich. Unless a village had a railway station, or a horse-drawn omnibus

Buses in the 1920s were often used for outings, like this one – probably to the seaside. The Chevrolet has locally-built bodywork, which was not unusual at the time

The title of the picture says it all – 'Motor Traffic', which is clearly taking the attention of this small Welsh town, as a Maudslay bus approaches

passing through, its isolation was as great as it had been for ages past, and the evidence of marriage registers shows how few people travelled far from their own parish. In-breeding produced the 'village idiot', and the fear of the work-house dominated the lives of the poor, not least because it meant in most cases a move to a distant and inaccessible place. For those who had occasion to travel, the roads were supplemented by a network of footpaths, and the distances that people walked would surprise their descendants of today.

Many journeys started and finished on foot, even if they involved the use of the train or the omnibus, or the carrier's cart, for part of the distance. But the villages were more self-sufficient than would be expected today, with butchers and bakers providing local supplies, and groceries being brought in by cart. The attraction of the market town lay in its lower prices, and it was the source of more durable necessities, like tools, implements and fabrics. Perhaps the first move to reduce isolation came after Forster's Education Act of 1870 began to make literacy more general, and increased the readership of local newspapers. Passenger transport is only one side of the story, and most people worked long hours for low wages, with little time or money to spare for 'gadding about'.

Not that there were no entertainments. Where chapel-going was strong, Sundays meant considerable distances to go to 'meeting', for the nonconformist 'Bethels' were often situated in isolated places, dating from an earlier period of

persecution. Not infrequently the family would take food for a picnic meal between the morning and afternoon services. The summer would see Sunday-school outings, riding in farm carts to a meadow where there would be games, and food and drink as well. Where the village was within reach of the coast, there might be an outing to the seaside, perhaps with a traction engine pulling the carts. There is a very long tradition of excursions that must have had as much social importance as the regular transport services for the village people.

In the late nineteenth century there arrived a new mechanical contribution to travel, in the shape of the bicycle. While for the middle classes it had a vogue as a means of touring, it opened new horizons for the countryside, making the journey to work easier for labourers and household staff, and — as the registers prove — extending the area within which people sought and found their marriage partners. In many a cottage the first and most essential mechanical devices would have been the sewing machine, and the bicycle.

Nevertheless, on the country roads at the eve of the motor age the horse still reigned supreme. In 1865 parliament had put an end to the serious development of steam traction on public roads, by the 'red flag Act', which required someone to walk in front of a heavy vehicle, bearing a flag, and which restricted the speed to as little as two miles an hour, depending upon its weight. George Ewart Evans has recorded in books like *The Pattern under the Plough* and *Ask the Fellows that Cut the Hay* the details of a whole way of life centred upon the horse, that has been swept away in a generation after lasting for perhaps 2,000 years. With it went the country roads of yesterday.

The changes in rural society that have marked the second half of our century have been due less to the motor vehicle and more to the development of agricultural machinery. These changes — at least the equivalent of the Industrial Revolution in its effect upon urban life — have been truly revolutionary, and in comparison the development of the country bus was a process of evolution. Combine harvesters were rare in 1945, when the rural bus services were approaching the peak of their prosperity. What is more, the buses were using roads, which — their surfaces apart — were largely unchanged, with high hedges and hedgerow trees in the south, and drystone walls in the north. Little wonder the buses remained small: even the maximum permitted width of 7ft 6in (2.3m) was too great for some roads in the Shropshire hill country.

The mechanisation of agriculture has had social consequences incomparably greater than the development of the motor bus, and though the consequent de-population has been offset to some extent by car-owning incomers and the sec-

Buses in the late 1920s, like this Dennis 'G' that ran between Rainham and Romford, were often small

A smart Bristol owned by a Surrey private operator waits to leave – followed by another

Roads in Wales have remained little changed, and even now the bus only just fits. A Bedford SBG of Mid-Wales Motorways provides a service to Brynlliwarch on the Newtown–Abermule circular on a Tuesday in 1977

ond homes of townspeople, the world that Bensusan described, the world in which Hardy's characters travelled the roads on foot or behind the horse, that world has gone for ever. Perhaps the loss to society has outweighed the gain; perhaps a yearning for times past accounts for the popularity of television serials such as *Emmerdale Farm* (which is near enough to real life to contain shots of real buses, usually almost empty).

The physical consequences of the agricultural revolution have been at least as great, and now that the industrialists of the fields have cut down the trees and grubbed out the hedges — changing in less than a generation the whole scale of the author's beloved East Anglia — it may not be easy to envisage the rural world into which the motor bus came. The secondary roads were little better than stabilised gravel, mended by tipping a load of hard-core where the pot-

The Leyland Lion in this picture, taken in 1932, belonged to Lincoln Corporation, but was well out in the country at the time

holes appeared. Minor roads were but cart-tracks between their walls or hedges, with three parallel ruts down them, one for the horse and one for each set of wheels. Passable in summer, they could be a barrier to communication in winter — no wonder Bensusan speaks of the road that 'divides' the villages of Great and Little Mudford.

The impact of motor vehicles on such roads gave rise to a great political problem. Local government reform in the late nineteenth century had placed road repair and maintenance in the hands of the councils, and (save for a few areas of the country, such as parts of South Wales) the turnpike system had been dismantled. The limited resources of local government were insufficient to meet the greatly increased costs imposed by motor traffic, which soon began to destroy the road surfaces. Faster than the steam or horse-drawn vehicles, the

Second-hand buses have always been found on country services. These three are all former London General 'B-types', owned in the early 1920s by a Bedfordshire operator, J. H. Pope, trading as Reliance, of Hockliffe. This was his entire fleet

Left, top. Country buses had little enough competition when this picture was taken in Peterborough

Left, bottom. Some time in the 1930s, the photographer has caught this Eastern Counties saloon resting on its way along the Norfolk coast. It has the peculiar 'bible' destination indicator that the company favoured for many years

motors sent up clouds of dust in the summer, and turned roads into quagmires in winter, while regular motor traffic produced corrugations as well as pot-holes even in the better road surfaces. The nuisance caused a public outcry.

Road-users were up in arms at the problem as much as were the rural ratepayers, and none more so than the cyclists, for whom the country roads had become a place of recreation. Their spokesman was W. Rees Jeffreys, a remarkable man who, by 1914, had visited every major art gallery in Europe — on a bicycle. He became Secretary of the Road Board set up by Lloyd George in 1909, and was able to channel some of the funds obtained from the new petrol tax to road improvement. It is to his efforts that we owe much of the impetus that produced the 'road revolution' of the years just before and after World War I.

The problem was to find a way of sealing the surface of the existing roads, so as to make them impervious to water and frost, which can together commence a process of disruption that wheeled traffic will quickly extend. The use of water to lay the summer dust did little to help the winter problem, and the experiments with oil as a binding substance proved disastrous — it combined with other substances to produce a colloid in which the wheels of vehicles could find no purchase. While asphalt and concrete surfaces were effective in towns, they were too expensive for country roads, and the solution eventually found was to use hot tar as a seal for the 'macadamised' road, binding this in turn with shingle or granite chips — producing what we know as tarmac. With considerable speed the whole network of secondary roads and many minor ones as well had been treated by the middle of the 1920s, just when the buses were spreading through the countryside.

Even so, the speed with which the work was done varied from one part of the country to another. The history of Laycocks, the Yorkshire pioneer business we met with in the previous chapter, tells that it was 'late in 1929' that the road between Salterforth and Barnoldswick was metalled, and this combined with a new bridge across the Leeds & Liverpool canal led the firm to start a local service on Christmas Eve of that year.

Just what country people thought about it all is less than well recorded, but there was one country gentleman who was walking along a Suffolk road one day when a car stopped, and one of its occupants asked him the way. He and his colleague, he said, were examining a possible bus route for the Eastern Counties Road Car Company, of Ipswich, and having received their instructions they drove off in a cloud of dust. Our friend waved his stick at them, and made uncomplimentary remarks — but his son, who was with him and who tells the story, was to become a well-known East Anglian bus operator himself. Certainly the service proved welcome to the villagers who supported it.

Macadamised roads demanded the application of carefully graded stones, and the spread of tarmac put an end to one rural occupation. 'Stonecracker John', as a contemporary song called him[1], had sat by the road with a hammer and an iron ring, grading the road metal, watching all those who came and went about their own occasions. Now only his companion the roadman was left, clearing drains and tidying the edges of the tarmac, seeing the new-fangled vehicles pass by, and keeping his own counsel. But the roads had been made fit for the traffic that used them.

1 This would be the same man that Yeats had in mind, when he wrote:
  Parnell came down the road, and said to a cheering man —
  Ireland shall have her freedom, and you'll still be breaking stone.

4 Beginnings and Growth

Speaking of the way roads were maintained in medieval times, Jackman says that this was 'not considered as merely worldly, but rather as pious and meritorious work before God, of the same sort as visiting the sick or caring for the poor; men saw in this work a true charity for certain unfortunate people, namely, travellers'. It is possible perhaps to trace a link between this and the start of the first rural bus service, in December 1898, in Northamptonshire, for the historian of the period, E. S. Shrapnell-Smith, says that 'Dr E. H. Hailey . . . in conjunction with Mr W. Carlisle MP . . . *in order to aid local people,* started a service of vehicles each carrying from eight to twelve passengers between Newport Pagnell and Olney'[1]. This was not long after the first motor bus service had been started in Edinburgh, on 19 May 1898, and eight months before the first such service in London. The 'red flag Act' had been repealed in 1896, an event celebrated each year by the veteran cars' run from London to Brighton.

This service sounds as if it was more like an omnibus than a carrier's cart that connected the two little market towns in the valley of the River Great Ouse. Over the next twenty years the provincial bus network slowly began to spread — though it was not until the 'roaring twenties' that buses came to serve large parts of the countryside — and it would be wrong to see it as just a better class of carrier. With the new century there began a remarkable growth of investment, which, when World War I was over, was to take on the scale of a mania. The various elements that were involved deserve a mention, for they contributed several different traditions, with consequences that we can still detect today.

First, the railways — or some of them. As already seen the Great Western started to run motor buses in 1903, in response, the chairman told shareholders, to 'motor cars' which 'outside persons were successfully operating'. (There is a sense of GWR effortless superiority about that 'outside persons'.) For a railway company the motor bus offered an alternative to the expensive and speculative construction of a branch line, and in at least one case (the GWR branch from Lampeter to Aberaeron) the success of the bus justified its replacement by a light railway. In Suffolk the Great Eastern had long been pressed to build a branch from Ipswich to the mouth of the Orwell at Shotley, and while the GER directors had a history of caring for the rural economy, they must have been relieved to be able to provide a bus service instead, using remarkably heavy petrol-driven vehicles that were built in the company's works at Stratford. C. F. Klapper's comment on the Great Western can be applied to most of the railway companies that ran buses: 'Although expenses tended to exceed revenue the

---

1 Author's emphasis.

Silver Star is the fleet name of Thomas of Upper Llandwrog, whose ex-Eastern National Bristol SC4LK is leaving Caernarvon for Cesarea

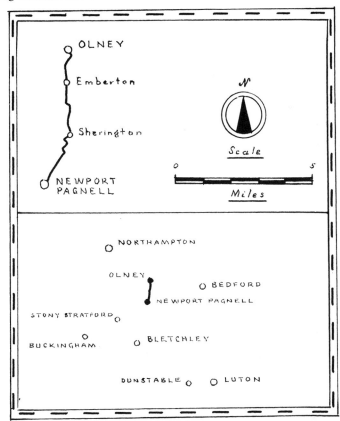

The first country motor bus route

At Cromwell Street Bus Station – if the title is justified – at Stornoway in 1982, the Harris Garage Company's bus waits to leave for Tarbert and the ferry to Skye

railway thought this well worth while if it saved capital expenditure on rural railway extensions' (*Golden Age of Buses*, p43).

Later the GWR developed more ambitious road services, the longest being Banbury–Swindon, via Chipping Norton, Burford and Lechlade, which in turn connected at Burford with a railway bus between Oxford and Cheltenham. Eventually it became a 'territorial operator', whose buses were no longer mere extensions of the train service; it was the only railway company to achieve this status, the others running more or less isolated services — most of them, however, strictly rural. Other interests developed the main network, as we have seen. The Great Western, incidentally, made no attempt to build its own buses, concentrating in the pre-war years upon the Milnes-Daimler, and then in 1925 buying no fewer than eighty small, fast Burfords — a maker's name now quite forgotten.

One consequence of the growth of rural bus services, whether railway-owned or not, was to preclude the development of rural light railways such as were common in France and Belgium. But the legal status of the railway buses was not always sound. Certainly the GWR had no statutory powers when it began to run on the roads, and Charles Lee states that at one time the big provincial bus companies considered challenging it in the courts, but decided that no good would come of such a move, since the services were so obviously useful. In 1928 the four main lines obtained powers to provide road motor transport, and the outcome of this was their purchase of up to 49 per cent of the shares in the large 'territorial' bus companies, to whom the railway bus services were then (in 1929) transferred. This in turn accounts for the rarity of rail-replacement bus services (at least until the Beeching cuts of the 1960s), and the absence of mixed road and rail operation, as practised abroad.

There was one exception to this, which, however promising it seems to have been, has remained a historical eccentricity. In 1930 the LNER closed all the intermediate stations between York and Scarborough apart from Malton and Seamer, and arranged for the villages to be served by the buses of United Automobile Services (without subsidy, be it said). In consequence the rail traffic between Leeds and Scarborough so increased as to require new platforms to be built at the seaside station. Just why this successful experiment was never repeated is still an unsolved mystery.

The provincial bus companies that became associated with the railways in 1929 played a great part in the establishment of the country bus. This was discussed in chapter two. They certainly served the villages, but it is hard to see them as rural bus operators, for they were town-based, and their main business was running

Caught here in the 1950s, this Jennings Leyland Cub dated from 1931, and had received a Perkins oil engine some 20 years later

A Lancia seems to be lurking in the shade at Ross-on-Wye, in early bus operating days

The timbers of Ledbury's Market Hall contrast with the austere lines of Tippings' austerity Bedford OWP, picking up passengers on a wet afternoon

inter-urban services that just happened to pass through the villages along the main roads. Not a few of them — Potteries Motor Traction is a good example — were in effect urban operators proper (Potteries was originally a tramway company), that happened to have a fringe of inter-urban services. Just as we saw Tony Weller in *Pickwick Papers* to be a townsman, so the bus drivers and conductors working for these companies were strangers to the villages they served. What is more, they worked (and mostly still do) on a rota basis, giving them no continued interest in the routes they might cover only once in every six weeks. There can be no greater contrast than that between the big inter-urban company, whose managers must make do with poor intelligence concerning their country services and the small business where the guv'nor is kept closely in touch — and may drive on the services himself.

Nevertheless, these big companies came to dominate the industry to a remarkable extent, not least because parliament in 1930 set up a licensing system for bus services that gave monopoly rights to those operators already in existence. A great consolidation of ownership then took place, and while it was accompanied by a much-needed tightening up of operating standards and maintenance, it had in general a deteriorating effect upon country bus services. Everywhere in Britain the small firms found they had a saleable business (though some of them got little enough for the goodwill), and in the territorial companies they found purchasers. This in its turn was in part the result of railway policy, for the big four companies made it plain they wanted to see such acquisitions, providing their associated bus companies with more than £9 million for the purpose.

There is an interesting comment on this in the memoirs of W. J. Crosland-Taylor, who went on managing his family business, Crosville Motor Services, after it was acquired, first by the LMSR, then by the combine, and finally by the British Transport Commission (Crosville remains one of the biggest territorial companies). He doubted very much whether it was wise to buy small businesses in North Wales that involved so much dead mileage when their services were operated from depots in places like Rhyl, and he went on to admit that he had to overcharge passengers in the Wirral in order to subsidise those in rural North Wales. But the policy of the big bus companies after 1930 was spend, spend, spend.

Sad to say, whenever a territorial bus company took over the services of a rural operator, the passengers felt that they were losing a friend. If the depot was big enough to be retained as an outstation there would be continuity among the drivers and conductors, but the past thirty years have seen the progressive closure of small depots and outstations, and the concentration of services upon the larger towns. This may have made sense to the accountants, but its disastrous consequences for the customers (and so for the companies themselves) can be readily imagined. (It is only fair to add that the last few years have seen the start of a new policy of decentralisation on the part of the territorial companies.)

This Bedford SB5, bought new by its owner, was ready to leave Bedford Square, Tavistock, when the picture was taken five years later, in 1973

The attitude of the big company managers could at times be reminiscent of robber barons. O. C. Power, the fiery Irish traffic manager of Midland Red, for long the largest of the provincial companies, had as his motto 'get off my route'. Crosland-Taylor recalls his father threatening to drive a small competitor off the road, and then virtually doing so. Charles Klapper once told me that Sir J. Frederick Heaton, the chairman of the Tilling Group, which came to own many of the most rural of the big companies, was 'a combination of a genius and a megalomaniac', and it seems to me that some deeper drive than the maximisation of profit lay behind the policies of the big companies' management. Why else should they have spent so much money to so little financial benefit — Crosland-Taylor's doubts as to the wisdom of buying small rural operators could be illustrated over and over again, all over the country. Yet there were also cases — Southdown Motor Services is a good example — where a large company, brilliantly managed in this case by A. D. Mackenzie, a busman of true genius, could establish a network of services so good that few smaller firms were attracted to compete.

There is a very good example of the whole attitude and process in the case of the family business of Gourds, at Bishopsteignton, in Devon. From their home village, Gourds ran to Teignmouth and to Newton Abbot, having started by carrying a few passengers in a pony and trap that had been bought to carry an unusual traffic — laundry baskets between the big houses in Teignmouth and the farms in Bishopsteignton where the washing and ironing was done. A few passengers began to be carried among the baskets, at 4d a time.

In due course the family obtained a motor bus — in this case as early as 1914. By the time the new licensing system came into force, in the spring of 1931, they had three buses, and were in competition with the Devon General, a territorial company partly owned by the Great Western and Southern Railways. From them they faced strong opposition when they applied for a road service licence, despite the supposed advantage of having 'grandfather rights' — that is, of having been the first operator on the road. Now one might think that the grant of their licence would have settled the matter, but in 1949 Devon General took Gourds back to the traffic court to claim that the larger firm had prior traffic rights over the section of road between Kingsteignton and Newton Abbot, and so Gourds must be made to double their fare over this stage, to 'protect' their competitors. (This was standard practice under the licensing system — whoever had priority could expect protection.)

Despite the increase, passengers still chose to use Gourds' buses, and the family made an issue of the matter, with banners on the sides of their vehicles

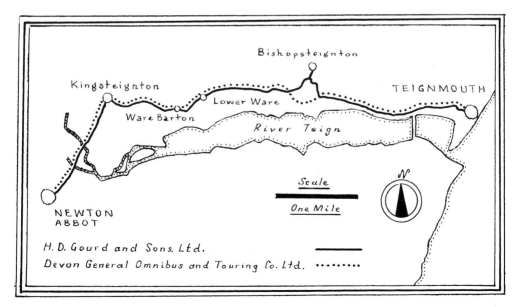

With Plymouth in the background, the Millbrook Steamboat & Trading Company's bus waits for the ferry to arrive

calling for fair fares. Whether or not this irked the Devon General managers we may never know, but there followed a most remarkable development, in which Mr Philip Gourd was pressed to sell out. The family was loath to do so — there are real satisfactions in running a business that is part of the community it serves — but eventually the price they were offered was too generous to refuse. Even the Devon General's solicitor asked why they had been paid 'such a ridiculous price'. And so, on 1 January 1951, another independent business was taken over, with the management of the service removed to Exeter. Whether it was a wise investment for the British Electric Traction Company, which owned the controlling interest in Devon General, it is hard to say, but it is at least possible that local management, and especially the lower costs of the smaller business, might have enabled the service to stand up better in the economic blizzard that hit the bus industry not long after it was taken over.

Where the private firms tended to survive was along the boundaries of the territorial operators, and in the 'thin' country such as Mid-Wales and the marches, or central Norfolk. (An interesting exception to this has always been south Durham, where small firms have long provided for the needs of the pit villages.) A series of 'area agreements', that started when the East Kent and Maidstone & District companies sought to define their respective territories in 1916, came to divide the whole country up, to the satisfaction of railway and big company managers, with tidy minds. The organisation that resulted has shown signs of strain in recent years, and the distinction between the big company with a few rural services and the country bus operator has become increasingly plain.

The difference is not just in scale. The large operator tends to think in terms of a network, while the small firm's individual services are easier to distinguish and understand. The average size of business in the whole independent sector — which includes a lot of urban coach operators — has stayed around five vehicles or a bit less for many years now, which may indicate that it doesn't pay to be big. In fact a lively and effective manager can maintain the sort of detailed interest that brings success over a fairly large number of services, but the trend has been for lively and effective managers to prefer the career structure and pension prospects of the big firms, and so the small firms, often family-run, have tended to stay small.

One-man one-bus firms, like the one that used to have a service once each way, once a week, between the Norfolk village of Little Hautbois and North Walsham, have always been rare. (Yes, there really is such a village, which you might have thought to have been invented by a novelist such as Margery Allingham.) Such a very small business needs to be associated with some other gainful activity, like keeping a pub. Rather more typical is the business run until recently under the name of its founder, B. K. Jennings of Ashen, in north Essex.

Mr Jennings, the son of a farmer in County Cork, came to England on holiday in 1922, and stayed. He married a girl from Essex, and bought a taxi, his

For years, Colchester town council provided a 'bus park' – no one would have called it a bus station. This Leyland from Plymouth Corporation has found its way to an Essex firm during the heady post-war years when country bus routes warranted double-deckers

53

health having prevented him from following a career in medicine. In 1923 he bought a bus, and obtained some contracts for schoolchildren's services (in those days they would be to secondary schools, for the village primary school was still everywhere to be found). Worked in with these he started services to the local market towns: to Braintree on Wednesdays, Sudbury on Thursdays and Haverhill on Fridays. This part of Essex lies on the borders of Eastern Counties and Eastern National operations, and independent firms are still significant there; by a sort of unspoken agreement, the villages have been shared out between them, and since the traffic has never been substantial there has never been much incentive to attract outside competition.

Only in one way is the Jennings business different from the general pattern of country bus operation, and that is in having as its principal route a daily, long-distance service to London. This was suggested by a neighbouring operator, who had started a successful London service from Halstead and the Hedinghams, and it was commenced in 1930, just in time to qualify for a road service licence when these came to be required. East Anglian railways tend to run across country, making roundabout journeys necessary to get to London from places

Nothing stirs on Angel Hill at Bury St Edmunds on a Sunday afternoon in 1963, as Rule's and Theobald's buses wait for the passengers whose numbers are already declining

as little as forty miles from the city, and Jennings was able to take advantage of this, running from the Stour Valley villages of Cavendish and Clare across through Thaxted to the A11 at Bishop's Stortford, and so up to town. One consequence was that for many years there were villages in north Essex that had a daily service to London, yet were connected to the nearest market town only once a week.

Jennings, like quite a few private operators, had an interest in the unusual, and in 1949 he obtained a Leyland Olympic 40-seater bus, one of very few of this early underfloor-engine design to be used in this country. Obviously satisfied, he subsequently bought another, with coach seating for the London service. Apart from this, he always had an interesting mix of vehicles; by the 1950s the bigger operators were busy standardising their rolling stock, but the small firms provided a fascinating assortment, reflecting a personal involvement in 'purchasing policy' that would be impossible within the management structure of the larger firms.

The size of Jennings' fleet has varied, being generally a little larger than average, with from six to eight coaches. The drivers know everyone on the road, and everyone knows the drivers, and Barnabas himself drove regularly up to and even after retirement. He told me once that he had deliberately refused to let the business grow any larger than he felt he could manage, and that is no doubt part of its success. For in such a business it is unthinkable to miss a journey, unless for the most serious weather conditions, and each service is watched over as if it were one's own offspring. This is not meant as a condemnation of the bigger firms — it is just that they are not organised to pay so much attention to detail.

Only too often, when small businesses have been acquired by the territorial operators, standards have slipped. When a service runs once a week, a missed journey is a disaster to people who have come to depend upon it, and this may not be as clear as it should to managers who are used to services that run every half an hour. There have even been cases where town-based drivers have lost their way in country lanes that their rota takes them to so rarely. Thus it is not just a sentimental attitude to praise the country bus firm, but a respect for the virtues of good business practice, all too often forgotten because success goes so easily unnoticed. It is worth recording here that the Jennings business in due course passed to its manager, Mr H. S. Springett, so that continuity, that all-important factor of success, was maintained. (In 1985 it was acquired by Mr Donald MacGregor.)

When B. K. Jennings started his business, buses were small — and this was partly because the roads were too narrow to take large ones. Before 1914 there had been a relative shortage of vehicles, and a serious shortage of drivers and fitters. It would be hard to exaggerate the consequences of World War I in permitting the rapid growth of the bus industry, both rural and urban, that immediately followed it. The war had been the first major conflict in which motor transport played a part, and a significant one at that. In the pre-war years the military had recognised its importance, offering subsidies to firms that bought vehicles to required specifications so that they could be quickly mobilised when the need arose. Suitable vehicles were requisitioned when war broke out, and in some places, like north Warwickshire, services had to be suspended — in that case they were taken over by Midland Red, whose petrol-electric buses were not acceptable to the War Office, a fact which contributed no little to the establishment of the company throughout the towns and villages of the Midlands. Eventually, in 1916, petrol for new bus services was no longer available, and the industry remained stable until the end of the war.

Then the floodgates were opened. Although motor buses had become fairly common by 1916, they were still rare in the Westcountry, those of the GWR apart; uncommon in the south Midlands and East Anglia; and absent from central Wales and Lincolnshire. In the north of England and Scotland they were widely scattered, and they were virtually unknown in Ireland. Ten years later the British Isles had an almost complete network of bus services, and long-distance coach services were about to flourish. None of this would have been possible if the licensing system had been introduced a decade earlier than it was.

For this growth, two things were necessary: the existence of demand and the availability of supply. There is very little information as to why there should have been sufficient demand, but it presumably had been there for a long time. Perhaps the promise of 'a land fit for heroes to live in' encouraged people to think more of travel, while certainly there was — for a time — more money about than there had been before the war. But most of the generalisations we do have concern the growth of urban and inter-urban travel, and all that we can say about the country bus is that country people welcomed it. Farm labourers still earned dreadfully low wages, but prices were lower in the market town, especially when the stalls were being taken down late in the evening, and perishable produce was sold off cheap, in the absence of refrigerators. So long as the bus fare was low enough, it made good sense to spend on travel in order to save on food, and perhaps to take a rabbit or two or a few pots of jam to sell. The bus offered also the occasional outing to the bigger city or the seaside, because it could go faster and further than any other form of transport except the train.

To satisfy this demand the end of the war produced a surplus of supply. At Slough and elsewhere there were great dumps of military vehicles for sale by auction, and a bit of ingenuity could provide a bus body for the stripped-down chassis of even an army lorry. Military training had produced capable fitters and mechanics, and more men (and women) than ever before had learned to drive in the forces. What is more, there were gratuities for the returning servicemen that could be invested in setting up in business. Many a butcher's shop or shoemaker started with money like that, and so did many a country bus service. Some of them failed, but many survived, and they gave steady employment to others, including another generation of men leaving the land when the Depres-

Not much luxury seems to be promised by this Chevrolet of a Mr J. Goates, who established himself on the 'back road' between Bedford and Cambridge – it dates from approximately 1924/25

A rare bird indeed – an AJS of Roberts Pioneer service, about to leave Newport for Fishguard, probably in the early 1930s

At Salisbury, the independent firms use The Canal, pictured here, as a terminal. The double-decker was originally with Hull Corporation Transport

sion came. For those who hadn't the wish for the risks of business, there was work with these firms, or, for that matter with the larger ones that were expanding fast at the same time.

There came, too, the manufacturers, seeking to establish their markets. Many of them were foreign, not the least important being the Ford Motor Company, whose Model 'T' laid the foundations of many successful firms (Mr Jennings' second bus was a Model 'T'). Another import from the USA was the Reo, of which some examples survived World War II. Leyland and other major firms were as ready to sell to small firms as to large, but Commer, Ford and Morris-Commercial were typical of the country bus fleet, along with Dennis and Austin. Between 1926 and 1937 the Gilford was a very popular make with independent operators, largely in the south, while Albions were by no means limited to their native Scotland. Many country firms combined freight and passenger work, and some of them had dual-purpose vehicles, whose chassis were capable of carrying a bus body one day and a van or lorry the next. There was even one firm in Essex which used the same vehicle as both a bus and a hearse: passengers, both living and dead, entered by a door at the rear.

To imagine the flavour of country buses in the years between the wars, and for some years after 1945 as well, we should picture a small vehicle, seating from 20 to 29 passengers, with seats in pairs and a central gangway. The driver sits inside with the passengers, and we enter by a doorway with two fairly steep steps. The door itself slides, or perhaps it may be a 'jack-knife' arrangement, with a lever that the driver can use to open and close it without leaving his seat (we really ought to say 'his or her' seat, for women have driven buses from the early days).

The driver sits behind the engine, which is housed in a bonnet, rather like a private car, only bigger — this is called 'normal control', in contrast to 'forward control', where there is a driver's cab, and he sits above and to the right of the engine. The steering-wheel is at an oblique angle, whereas in the case of forward control it is horizontal; this makes the bus easier to handle, and is a blessing on the narrow and twisting country lanes. The only other controls are the choke and self-starter on the dash, and the handbrake and gear levers, one on either side of the driver's seat. Instruments are limited to a speedometer with a mileage indicator — the latter not always to be found in the bigger buses — and an ammeter registering 'charge' or 'discharge' to the battery, but then the popular cars of the day had little more.

To such a fleet there would be added a few larger coaches, such as the one we met in the first chapter. With them the country bus entered a period of considerable prosperity, in the years from 1945 to 1955 or thereabouts. But the odd thing is still that its name is a misnomer, for our journey would have been made in a vehicle that was very definitely a *coach*. In that sense, the country *bus* can hardly be said to have existed.

Be that as it may, the rural bus companies contributed a great deal to the betterment of life in the countryside. Even where there was a railway station, people found that instead of having to walk to the train, the bus stopped at the door, and many roadside cottages came to have public transport available that for years had only heard the trains go by. Many British towns have badly placed stations, too, and the buses would set passengers down and pick them up in the market-place. How many thousands of journeys were made easier, less tiring and less fraught, we can never calculate, but all this adds up to answering the question, why was the bus so popular?

While there are examples in plenty of buses continuing the carriers' practice of 'putting up' at an inn, the expansion of bus services after 1919 brought with it a considerable increase in frequency on many inter-urban routes. No longer did the bus stand idle until it was time to take its passengers home; in order to increase paying mileage and to improve the service to the public, operators looked for ways of keeping their buses moving all day. But whereas urban buses usually allow a break for their crews at the outer ends of the routes, inter-urban and rural services must allow 'layover' in the towns they serve, so that the crews can get a break, and the bus be seen to be ready to depart — in publicity terms, the bus is its own advertisement.

In this way there grew up a need for some kind of bus station, though there was never a close similarity between bus stations and railway stations, for the railway station is also part of the administrative structure of the railway. In some places there was an open space, conveniently sited, that the bus operators could 'colonise' — Angel Hill, in Bury St Edmunds, or the Canal in Salisbury are good examples. In other places, where a large company came to dominate the services, it would provide its own terminal, as Eastern National did at Chelmsford. After 1929 there were a few cases where railway-associated companies were permitted to use station forecourts, but this was much rarer than might be expected. The sole use of a terminal could give the company a competitive edge over any remaining independents — at Halstead the Eastern National used the station forecourt, and nothing in their publicity indicated that the gaps in their timetable for the Colchester service were filled by Blackwell's bus, which ran from the Bull, just round the corner, but out of sight.

In some towns, though, a far-sighted council provided space for a terminal, usually charging a small fee per departure for its use. It is surprising how rare this has been, until we reflect upon the fact that country bus operators, in particular, are seldom ratepayers in the towns they serve. Even so, it might have been expected that a council would recognise the trade that the buses brought in, and at least provide an area of hardstanding and a waiting room, as Colchester did in the 1920s. (Though even at Colchester there were two private firms still using inn yards as late as the 1950s, before the old 'bus park' was replaced by a 'bus station', with platforms and more sophisticated accommodation for the public.)

We shall see in chapter eleven how the planners in the past thirty years have shown a sad tendency to move the buses away from the town-centre terminals that provided part of their attraction, usually in order to make more room for the private car. In some of our larger cities — such as Newcastle upon Tyne and Nottingham — there has been specific development of bus stations, but the smaller market towns do not on the whole have such a good record. For the

Some years after the previous picture was taken, The Canal is not even restricted to buses – despite the sign – and the buses are notably smaller

shopper, the cardinal attraction of the bus has to be its capacity to take you from door to door, and it was upon this that its early success was built.

Its other contributions must not be neglected, either. It increased the opportunity for leisure travel, as we have seen; it made secondary education possible for village children, often for the very first time; and it improved access to employment. By the same token, it attracted people to come and live in the country, and contributed to that scourge of the 1930s, ribbon development. Its growth as a means of transport coincided with the start of rural depopulation, and its more recent decline has been connected with the great changes that have come over rural Britain in the past thirty years. In a sense, the arrival of the country motor bus foreshadowed the end of country life as it has been known for generations, and there comes to mind the melancholy of Goldsmith's *Deserted Village*:

And, trembling, shrinking from the spoiler's hand,
Far, far away thy children leave the land.

5 Mechanical Marvels

We have seen that the typical country bus is more than likely to be a coach. Once again, we should not forget the buses of the big companies, though, for they too serve the villages, and even they tended for a long time to provide a standard of comfort, and even decoration, that in recent years has been lost. Austerity has become the hallmark of public transport, though whether the public appreciates it is another matter — certainly it is not expected of the private car.

On such a scale the evolution of the country motor bus proceeded upwards from the omnibus and the carrier's cart to a high point in the 1930s — the Golden Age, as Charles Klapper defined it — and it has since entered a decline. World War II saw a sharp falling-off, bringing slatted wooden seats, and the 1950s saw a major change with the introduction of successful underfloor engines; even today, a further change is taking place, as the new breed of super-coaches enters the top end of the market. Compared with these, the vehicles of the past seem to belong to a different world.

Greenslades of Bradninch, in Devon, ran this MASS with charabanc body as early as 1914

By far the most common country bus in the early days was the Model 'T' Ford, like this one – which cost about £275 complete. It belonged to J. C. Parnell's Haddenham & District business in Cambridgeshire

The first motor buses simply had the motor where the horse would have been. Those little vehicles that plied between Olney and Newport Pagnell would probably have been 'motor waggonettes', and we may suspect that their lightness would have given people a rough ride if they made any speed. To start with, improvisation was the order of the day; the first GWR buses — the ones that came from the Lynton & Barnstaple — were Milnes-Daimlers of 16hp, with 22-seat waggonette bodies incorporating luggage accommodation. Many early buses in railway ownership had a distinct resemblance to the railway carriage (some of them were in fact steamers, such as the Clarksons on the Chagford route of the LSWR). The Midland built some buses for its Northern Ireland business, the Northern Counties Committee, which had characteristic roof ventilators of standard Derby pattern.

Having started very light, buses then tended to get over-heavy, and it was not until 1919 that the difference between the country bus and the rest began to appear. The real cause of the difference lies in the annual mileage expected of the vehicle, for the urban and inter-urban operators were looking for a motor bus that could compare with the tramcar in its reliability over a high mileage. Thus, as we saw in chapter one, the difference between the small country operator and the territorial company has been the tendency for the latter to use inter-urban buses on rural services. This however did not at first appear.

Another stand-by of the small firms of the 1920's was the Chevrolet. This one – somewhat run-down when the picture was taken – belonged to the Bluebird fleet of Hinds & Savage, of Luton

Another Chevrolet, at the end of its days. This one had belonged to Evans of Llanfihangel-yng-Gwynfa, near Llanfyllin – the picture was taken in 1969

The charabanc as it really was (and how can people use the word for today's coaches!)

The small firms of the 1920s established themselves with light and nippy buses, of which the Model 'T' Ford was typical. It was not unusual for them to be 14-seaters, which today is the capacity of many a minibus. Harry Rippingale, of Gestingthorpe, in north Essex, started in 1923 with a Model 'T', bought new, and six years later he obtained a Chevrolet, also new. This was a 14-seater, but a 20-seater arrived in 1931, second-hand from Hicks Brothers (a much larger family business); this was a Reo Gold Crown, which ran until 1953, when its body was put to further use as a hay store. He had a Lancia 16-seater for a time, and another Chevrolet, but after the war he concentrated, as did many others, upon Bedfords, several with the Duple coachworks body known as the Vista. One of these, though, was a 31-seater bus (rather than a coach), with a body by Mulliner — the biggest vehicle Rippingale ever owned. True to form, a 20-seater Bedford, bought second-hand from Osborne of Tollesbury, finished its life as a chicken-house.

These small firms have always tended to sell vehicles to each other, rather as the Irish tinkers are said to be always swapping asses, and this again distinguishes them from the 'respectable' operators. Many of them were owned by 'black-handed engineers', men who were as happy tuning the engine as they were in the driving seat — and far happier either way than they would have been behind a desk. For them, standardisation was not a serious problem, for they bought what they wanted when they needed it (or when they spotted a bargain), and they may well have valued the novelty of a different make of vehicle. Neither would this be mere eccentricity, but a genuine interest in the engineering side of the work. Few of them, on the other hand, were interested in complicated machines, for the simplicity of the petrol engines of those days contributed greatly to their ability to survive.

Rather heavier than the early buses were those coaches so characteristic of the 1920s, the charabancs. (I regard it as an affectation to ape the French original in forming the plural of so very English a word.) For a vehicle that has so totally gone out of existence — I know of none that has been preserved — the word has lingered on remarkably; it is the mark of a certain upper-class ignorance to call a modern coach a 'chara'. Neither is its use limited to the motor trade, for Irish children used the word to mean a swing, of the kind in which there are several seats at each end. In Liverpool it came to be applied to the people who travelled by coach, long after the vehicle itself must have been forgotten: someone would 'get up a chara to Blackpool lights'.

More properly called a 'torpedo', the chara was perhaps predominantly an urban vehicle, but it keeps appearing in old photos of village life. There will be rows of slightly self-conscious passengers, with as often as not the driver and one or two others, wearing caps, or even long white coats, looking rather blasé about the whole affair. The chara seated up to thirty people, in rows with doors at each end of the row, and a long running-board from which the doors gave entry to the seats. It is usually to be seen open to the winds of heaven, but with a big hood at the back, that could be brought forward to cover the passengers when it rained, an operation of considerable difficulty if there was wind as well. Hardly surprisingly, it gave way early in the 1930s to the 'saloon', although there remained a hint of it in the 'sunshine saloon', which had a long sliding roof, that could be opened when required.

Standing outside the village pub, ready to leave for Scarborough or Weston-super-Mare, the charabanc was novel — that buzz-word of the 1920s. Its weakness lay in being of little use for any kind of stage service, though there were a few so used, whose conductor had to cling to the running-board to get the fares, like the conductor on an Isle of Man horse tram. Country operators could hardly afford so specialised a vehicle, which probably accounts for its rapid and total disappearance, but the outing remained a lucrative part of the operators' business, so long as the coach could be used on all kinds of work. Thus there grew up the further distinction between the large and the small operators, for the small firms tended to use the coach as a bus, while the large ones were sometimes — rather mistakenly, to be sure — known to use a bus as a coach.

In the 1930s, though, comfort and elegance reigned. 'Art deco' of the kind associated with the picture palaces of the period combined with the development of really comfortably upholstered seats to produce the luxury coach, and where rural operators could afford to, they bought it. Many of the large inter-urban operators followed the same policy, while of course their activities in buying out their competitors brought numbers of non-standard vehicles into their fleets.

The Construction and Use Regulations introduced under the Road Traffic Act of 1930 dominated the design of public service vehicles thereafter in many ways, but not least in the maximum 'box dimensions'. These were 7ft 6in (2.3m) wide by 27ft 6in (8.4m) long; if there were three axles the length might be 30ft (9.1m). The effect was to limit the seating capacity of the vehicle, especially

This stylish Edwardian conveyance was in fact a steamer, built by Clarkson and paraffin-fired. The upper deck accommodation appears to be a couple of park benches

since there were further regulations that governed the distance to be set between the seats. In practice, the typical small rural coach, such as we looked at in chapter four, was shorter than the permitted length, while C. F. Klapper records that some Shropshire operators in the 1930s had buses 6ft 6in (2m) wide, 'to minimise damage in narrow lanes' (*Golden Age of Buses*). A further regulation prescribed that no conductor need be carried on a bus with twenty seats or less, so it is not surprising that country buses at this time remained small.

Even so, the 'bigger' vehicles were not all that large, for the half-cab, forward control coaches that became more common throughout the 1930s seldom seated more than thirty-two. This was due partly to the size of the seats, for the same dimensions later on permitted manufacturers to produce 35-seaters within the same 27ft 6in (8.4m) length, by using lighter frames and thinner upholstery. Coaches of the golden age, though, really were comfortable; memory may play me tricks, but in my opinion they greatly outclassed those of the 1970s. (I say this because the super-coaches of today, and still more some that I have seen in South America, are setting new standards entirely.) Clocks were often mounted on the bulkhead, facing the passengers, and by the end of the period there were heating devices for the winter. Curtained windows were usually more for decoration than anything practical, but upholstery in leather was giving way to cut moquette, usually carried up the side walls, along the undersides of the luggage

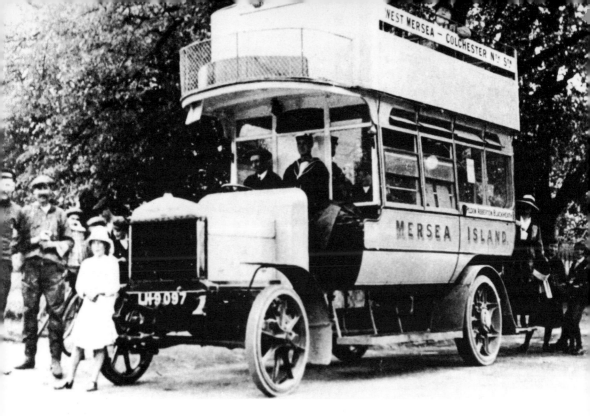

A former London Straker Squire exiled to W. Mersea. Chassis of 1913 vintage, photographed c1921

racks, and on the ceiling. That hangover from the Edwardian era, the anti-macassar, was to be found on many seats, though it was only the top-flight coach firms, invariably city-based, that went so far as to have the operator's initials embroidered on them.

These coaches had windows that really opened, usually with winding handles like those of a private car. The law requires an emergency door that must not be on the same side as the normal entrance — for obvious reasons — and this came to be placed usually on the offside, at the opposite end of the vehicle. Emergency doors at the rear meant the loss of a seat — it is the full width back seat that accounts for the tendency for the coaches of the period to be licensed to carry an odd number of passengers. (On late evening journeys, the back seat also acquired the same reputation as the equivalent position in a cinema.)

The door itself was usually at the front, but this was by no means the rule. Even front entrance doors were often placed behind a pair of seats that gave uninterrupted views forward. A rear entrance was very unusual in normal control vehicles, and a considerable nuisance for the operator of stage services, since it made a conductor obligatory. A door in the centre was not unknown on forward control coaches, but it was more usually to be found at either the front or the back. (The latter position largely disappeared in the final, post-war generation of forward control coaches, but it was by no means uncommon in the 1930s — it tended to make for a very draughty back seat.)

Doors, as we shall see, have their problems. Jack-knife doors, more commonly found on the small normal control vehicles, meant an awkward entrance, for part of the integral step had to be cut away to allow the necessary movement. Hinged doors, opening outward, were to be found on some early touring coaches, but they were dangerous in stage service use, and their weight caused them too easily to get out of balance. By 1939 the sliding door was almost universal for forward control vehicles, and the standard 26/29-seater normal control body typified by the product of the Duple works had the same provision. But any door on a large vehicle like a bus or coach must be heavy, and without regular inspection and greasing the mounting can easily get out of true, making it no easy matter to slide the door along. (An inescapable tendency for passengers to try to open sliding doors outwards contributes to the problem as well.) Modern super-coaches have automatic double jack-knife doors that escape these problems, which were by no means negligible in the golden age.

The only solution to the problem of the door was the presence of the conductor. But his (or her) job was always one that involved more than just collecting the fares — and still does, where that endangered species survives. From my own days working 'on the back' I recall a permanent sense of muscular strain in the right shoulder, caused by heaving the sliding doors to and fro. I recall, too, that it was not only the passenger door that required my attention: there was also the door of the boot.

Country passengers don't travel for the pleasure of it, however much the social aspect of the journey may please them. Their primary purpose is economic. They are doing the shopping. And because the prices in the village shop are higher than they are on market-day in the town, they tend to make a weekly shopping trip that contrasts with the urban habit of slipping round to the stores. (One-stop shopping in the supermarket age has brought this to the towns, at least for those who can afford it.) The bus passengers therefore start out with shopping bags and baskets, and if you have thirty-two passengers with an average of two bags each, you have an accommodation problem. But that is not all, for many of them will be young women with children under school age, and for each of these there will be a folding pushchair. Space has got to be found for all these objects, and that is why the country bus must always have a boot.

In the early days it was common practice to load such things on the roof — and I recall one day in 1952 setting out from Dublin for Avoca on a CIE[1] bus that was loaded up this way, with even a bicycle or two. (We had problems, though, because the relief was loaded the same way, but sometimes the people were in one bus, and their belongings on the top of the other — when the relief turned

1 CIE — the initials of Coras Iompair Eireann, 'Ireland's Transport Company', the state-owned canal, rail and road operator of the Republic of Ireland.

back at Newtownmountkennedy there was some complicated rearrangement required.) Conductors in those days needed climbing ability, and a friend on the ground to throw things up when loading, or catch them when the passengers were leaving the bus. Once more the vital significance of the boot is seen, which, for some reason, came to be ignored when the big companies started to standardise their fleets.

The country bus conductor, or the driver, if the bus is being worked 'd/c' (driver-conduct), needs a boot key. The door will have 'budget' lock, into which the squared-off end of a metal bar will fit, though proper T-shaped budget keys can be bought from an ironmonger. It is traditional for a slit to be cut in the strap of the cash bag to hold the boot key, for the cash bag is something from which the conductor can no more be parted than a woman from her handbag. Thus the key is always to hand when there are passengers joining or leaving the bus, for depend upon it, the boot will need to be opened — especially on the way home.

The other little job that has always been the responsibility of the conductor is changing the destination blind. No respectable vehicle in the 1930s but had a roller blind, mounted in a glass-fronted case built into the canopy, or set into the front above the driver's windscreen. The winding handle might be inside, in which case the driver would probably see to the matter, but on some forward control coaches and on most double-deckers it protruded somewhere outside, usually in such a position as to require climbing on the bumper or the wing, with due care to avoid painful contact with a hot radiator shell. In a small firm, the choice of destinations would be limited, and in any case, the journeys would be few enough for the very arrival of the bus in its familiar livery to indicate its objective to the passengers waiting by the village pump. If that were not enough, the driver would be well known to them, and since it would be he that brought them home, they would look for a familiar face as often as they might consult the indicator. But it was a matter of pride to have it set right.

So far we have been thinking of the coaches that ran so many of the country bus services before World War II. The bigger firms tended to provide something of the same quality of service, if without the personal touch, and where the villages were served by inter-urban buses they had many of the same facilities, even to the provision of a boot. In the 1930s the Eastern National company linked up various services to work through from Clacton-on-Sea or Harwich via Colchester and Chelmsford to Grays and Tilbury, and these hourly cross-country journeys, which catered for many intermediate villages, were worked with Dennis Lancet coaches with bodywork of considerable luxury. (The Lancet was well able to cope with the ascent of Langdon Hill with a full load, while the Bristol buses that succeeded them did not have the same reputation.) But even before the war, the double-decker was starting to reach the country routes, chiefly where these were served by the territorial companies.

Within the box dimensions, the very most that a single-decker could seat, and that in some discomfort, was 37 passengers, and most such buses, as we have seen, seated 35 or less. In comparison, a double-decker could seat 48, or even 53, and if this meant saving a relief, it was an economy not to be missed. Eastern National started allocating spanking new Bristol double-deckers to rural services in 1938, one of them going to the Dedham outstation, to work the service thence into Colchester, a country bus service if ever there was one. The outstation crew kept it in beautiful condition, and it was really a very superior vehicle, with semi-luxury seating in dark blue moquette — perhaps not entirely typical of the period, but very different from the austerity of the post-war rolling stock. At that time, though, very few private firms in the countryside were running anything but saloons.

The trouble with the double-decker turned upon the lack of a boot. The space under the stairs was never enough to hold all the pushchairs, let alone the shopping baskets, and passengers probably felt uncomfortable on the journey, in case anything should roll off the platform and away. Thus the conductor's job was complicated by having to negotiate the passengers' belongings placed in the aisle, as soon as there was anything like a load.

With the war years there came greatly increased demand, and while the government immediately put a stop to the construction of new buses, 'freezing' a number of chassis, it later permitted some of them to be released, and to be

For travellers in the roaring Twenties, this was unmistakably a bus. It is a Maudslay, and was owned by Goad Bros of Plympton, who traded as Ensign. At least the destination blinds never needed to be changed!

Silcox of Pembroke Dock owned this Guy 'B', which probably started life in a municipal fleet in the late Twenties

given 'austerity' bodies. But these were mainly for inter-urban services, and the true country bus remained little affected by the war. Blackout regulations were a problem, and spares became hard to find, while petrol for anything but stage operation was made increasingly scarce (express services, indeed, were suspended entirely). Some of the territorial companies introduced coke as a fuel, which was burned on trailers to make 'producer gas', but proved a very inefficient substitute for petrol, especially on hilly routes. (Old jokes were revived, such as 'first-class passengers get out and walk: second-class get out and push'.) What perhaps caused most inconvenience, though, was the invention of 'perimeter seating'.

I first met this method of packing in extra passengers when going from Bromeswell to Ipswich for an evening at the pictures, some time in the winter of 1943–4. The single-decker looked a typical Eastern Counties Leyland of the period: forward control, and a sliding door to the rear. Inside it was very different, for all the seats had been moved and set against the sides, and even against the bulkhead, leaving a kind of dance-floor in the middle, with metal tread-plates bolted to it at regular intervals. By the time we reached Woodbridge the seats were mainly full, but by the time we entered Ipswich the dance-floor was crowded — though nothing like as much as it was on the last journey home! How the conductress got the fares in remains a puzzle, not least because the only interior lighting consisted of a low-power bulb set in a sort of inverted jam-jar that could be drawn along a live metal strip fixed to the ceiling, by the use of a convenient piece of string. Yet without the crowds, it would have been a problem to stay on one's seat as the bus turned a corner.

Perhaps the war-time austerity, combined with the poverty of the nation in the post-war years, influenced the big companies' vehicle policy that gave us a period — not yet ended — when inter-urban and rural buses became positively uncomfortable to ride in. Perhaps this too has made the private car, or the taxi, a much preferred alternative — I wouldn't wonder. It must be admitted that not a few small firms have gone the same way, influenced partly by what the manufacturers have had on offer, partly by a certain tendency to ape the big boys. I suspect, though, that the chief influence latterly was the 'new bus grant' (now phased out) that was available to firms providing stage services, but that required them to buy vehicles that conformed to ministry specifications. And I very much doubt whether the clever boys in the ministry drawing offices had any notion of what country bus operation is about.

Before the bus grant, though, there came the biggest revolution in design since the earliest days of the bus, with the successful development of the under-floor-engined vehicle. Box dimensions were eased in the early 1950s to permit a width of 8ft (2.4m), which made room for more comfortable seats (or wider gangways), but the new vehicles that came on to the market at about the same time offered something more: the full permitted length could now be used for carrying passengers. Immediately the normal seating capacity went up to 41, with 43 or 45 possible at a squeeze, and immediately the forward control, half-cab coach was old-fashioned, not to say obsolete. Back in the 1930s, AEC had developed the 'Q', which had a side-mounted engine, but there were technical problems, and even the 'Q' tended to seat only thirty-two passengers or so. (There was a double-deck version, but that was very rare — the most familiar 'Qs' were coaches used by Green Line around London.) The secret of the un-derfloor engine was flexible mounting, and the development of pipework for fuel, lubricants and coolant, and much of the original work was done in the de-sign of diesel-mechanical railcars for the Great Northern Railway of Ireland. (The GNR also pioneered the automatic gearbox — I can recall the odd sensa-tion, for 1952, of hearing the gears change beneath me, travelling back from Howth to what was then still Amiens Street, in Dublin.)

Whereas the diesel engine had been used for coaches and buses from the early 1930s, its choice by small businesses remained unusual for at least another thirty years. This again reflects the distinction in terms of annual mileage, for the higher first cost of the diesel meant that its greater fuel economy did not give it an advantage over petrol under something like 20,000 miles a year. Few country bus firms achieved anything like this, and in any case the petrol engine retained the advantage of simplicity — skilled diesel mechanics commanded a good wage because of their scarcity. A lot of operators felt too that the petrol engine gave a much smoother ride, which was appreciated by passengers on private hire out-ings and tours. There was also the cost of providing separate tanks to store petrol and diesel, so that it seems hardly surprising that the petrol engine remained popular. Looking back, it seems that the biggest impact upon country operators was the withdrawal from the market in the late 1950s of the Bedford OB/Duple Vista 29-seater coach that was for the period of the post-war boom the work-horse of the rural independents, as we shall see in chapter ten.

In the 'golden age', passengers were pampered. They got the best standard of comfort that was available, in the new coaches that served the country routes in the 1930s. When you have been shopping, carrying your goods around, and coping with a couple of small children, you welcome the comfort of a deep, well-upholstered seat, to say nothing of a conductor — whose face is familiar, and whose family is well known to you — to help you get aboard. A hard, low-backed seat in a neat, well-designed, but basically unattractive vehicle, with a driver who may well be a stranger, and who doesn't turn up until it's time for the bus to go, is a poor substitute for comfort, familiarity, maybe a bit of a fug, and decoration which, however poor may be its taste in other eyes, is something you are used to and admire. Not a few of the small firms that survive in the deep rural areas seem well aware of this, and not a few of them still make a living, without even asking the earth in terms of subsidy. Successful operation of the country bus depends to quite a large extent upon the sort of country bus you run. It is probably still best if it is really a coach.

6 Down Country Lanes

Let us take another journey. It is a cold February morning in 1944, and we are waiting at the roadside where the Swan lies in the hollow, near Bromeswell Heath, in Suffolk. The plane overhead is a Flying Fortress, returning late from its mission, and making for the US airfield at Rendlesham, but the Americans — and indeed the war itself — might be far away. For it is Tuesday, Ipswich market-day, and Foreman's market bus is coming down the hill on its way from Orford.

A Ford of uncertain age, it can only be regarded as 'vintage', even by the standards of 1944. It is very square, with a ladder up the back to load luggage and goods into a sort of roofless cage on the top. Its paintwork is by no means new, and it is altogether removed from the sleek-looking Eastern Counties vehicle that is also due (even if the latter has got perimeter seating). But we hail Foreman's bus, and it stops for us to climb in. By no stretch of the imagination can it be called luxurious, but it is already fairly full, having stopped to pick up at Sudbourne, Chillesford and the Oyster at Butley on its way from Orford; the Swan will be its last stop till it reaches the Blue Coat Boy at Ipswich. It is actually fuller than it looks, because the back two pairs of seats have been removed, leaving space for more goods — as we find our own seats, we can see several boxes of cabbages, a quantity of dead rabbits and one live goat.

Foreman and Sharman, the two village carriers of Orford, had been licensed to operate their bus services, once weekly, when the law required it in 1931. It would take a stretch of the imagination to class them as bus operators like the Eastern Counties company, yet they too were filling a need, and in a fashion that was certainly bequeathed by the country carriers of untold generations before. On the return journey there would be groceries of various kinds, perhaps even rationed goods, for it paid people to register with market stall-holders, even for their meat and bacon. There would be rolls of wire netting on top, and rolls of linoleum inside, seed potatoes, a new spade, and batteries and accumulators for the wireless. Somewhere about five miles from the coast there would be a road-block, with British soldiers checking all vehicles, and turning back those with no business to go further, but Foreman's bus would not be delayed long, because no strangers ever found out where it went.

And so, in the growing dusk, the bus pulls up outside the Bromeswell Swan once more, the driver opens the jack-knife door, and hands us down our bags and baskets, amid a word and a wave from the people we know, and then we are left standing, the one weekly outing over, and the water to be drawn from the pump to make the tea. In every direction from Ipswich, similar journeys are ending (though few perhaps in buses quite as old as Foreman's), as they do

Presumably the dog knows where the driver has gone for his cup of tea, as the bus waits at Tolsta – one of Britain's lonelier terminals – to return to Stornoway, on the Isle of Lewis. It (the bus) is owned by William MacDonald, of Back

every Tuesday. On Monday it will have been Hadleigh — though few buses go there, it is such a small market; on Wednesday it will be Bury St Edmunds, that great attraction for buses from all over Suffolk; on Thursday rather fewer will be going to Stowmarket; the Friday market in these parts is over the Norfolk border, at Diss.

The market buses have always been superimposed upon the ordinary bus services, though in the more remote parts there may be the market bus and nothing else. Many of them have gone now — Foreman's and Sharman's among them, and the Swan is a public house no more — but many still remain. The importance of a market town can be measured very accurately by the buses that come into it on market-day: in East Anglia Bury St Edmunds is closely followed by Norwich in importance, with King's Lynn and Ipswich next in order. Many of the traders go from one place to another, and some of the bus passengers make a convivial day of it, for it is a peculiarity of the English liquor laws that the pubs stay open all afternoon in the vicinity of the market, on market-days (the same is true in Wales, where the market buses are just as much a part of the transport scene).

If you live in a village where a local firm has its garage, you may have the choice of several markets on different days of the week. In north Devon the market buses may go weekly to Barnstaple, and also monthly to Exeter, emphasising once more the subtlety of the hierarchy of market towns. During the boom years for country buses, from 1945 to 1960, many operators built upon the market-day demand and added journeys on other days, especially Saturday, but in recent years the growth of car ownership has tended to cut this back. If the family breadwinner has the car five days a week, it is available for Saturday's shopping, but the habit of going out on market-day has remained strong, and the market bus survives.

Part of the reason is purely social, however much the economics of the weekly shopping may influence demand. Gossip that would grace the pages of Mrs Gaskell is not unknown on the market bus, and this is meant in no derogatory sense, for it is just this sharing of each others' lives that knits villages together. Sometimes it may make problems, though, for neighbouring villages may share ancient feuds, which can make for embarrassment when the same bus serves them both.

The country bus, then, is a sort of community, no less real for being ephemeral, and full membership of it belongs to the driver and — when there is one — the conductor. The driver in particular must know the regular passengers, and look out for the stop at which they get on and get off. The first thing you need to un-

A sunny winter day in mid Wales, with a bus-bodied Bedford OB of Mid-Wales Motorways at the terminus of a market-day service from Newtown to Mochdre and Pentre. The year is 1970

Now then, young fellah, that there basket means yer stops down the lane at Rose Cottage 'n' 'onks twice!

derstand is that a regular passenger does not expect to have to hail the bus, and will more than likely be standing with her back to it, conversing over the garden fence with a neighbour. (This is just as likely to be true if the passenger is a man.) When I was running Corona Coaches we acquired Harry Rippingale's business, and I made a point of conducting all the routes myself, with Harry's driver, who we had also engaged. There was one lane at Belchamp Walter which we used only for one journey each way on Thursday afternoons (Sudbury market-day), and on which there was a farm, a pub and just one cottage. 'Guv'nor,' I was told, as we approached it, 'you want ter watch 'n see if there's a shoppin' bag on the gatepost — if there ain't they ain't a cumm'n.' Naturally the two ladies concerned rode with us that day, to try out the new bus firm, but I was able to pass the hint to the rest of the staff. I've often wondered what would have happened if Eastern National had taken over the service instead of us.

The second commandment is not to forget where your regulars get off, because they may be too much engaged in conversation to remind you. Charles Klapper has a story of riding with the proprietor of the Hope Valley Services of Bishop's Castle, who was driving on the Bishopsmoat circular when an old lady called out: 'Mr Carpenter, you've passed my turning.' The driver's response was immediate: 'Oh, we wouldn't want to do that, otherwise we'd have to keep you for a week!' — and on many such services the next bus would indeed be a

78

week later. (The Valley Services bus garage, Klapper records, was 'built out of the former Bishop's Castle railway station, and the service to Craven Arms took the place of the light railway which had been in the hands of a Receiver since 1868' — *Golden Age of Buses*.)

The driver on the country bus knows everybody, and takes a proper interest in strangers (or 'foreigners', as we call them in Essex). It is told of Laycock's business that the oldest member of the staff was a great talker:

Regardless of weather conditions, he would always turn round as he was driving to chat with his passengers, even if it was someone he had never seen before. He was always having his leg pulled about this, but was never known to have an accident. The two buses on the Skipton–Barnoldswick service passed each other at East Marton, but on one foggy night the bus to Skipton met Ted at Broughton [some miles short of where he should have been]. Ted had been talking again and upon reaching Niffney Corner, instead of following the main road on its sharp left-hand bend, had driven his vehicle on to the swing bridge over the canal, which leads to the farm.

One of the most striking characteristics of the country bus, as already suggested in my account of a journey to the Cotswolds in chapter one, is that its passengers mostly travel out and home on the same day, in the same bus, and with the same

The scattered population of Weardale, in County Durham, and the narrow roads too, account for the size of this 'baby Bedford' of the local operator, which is only 7ft 6in (2.3m) wide

crew. Its primary purpose is taking people to town, and at its simplest it does make just that one round trip. Where there is more traffic, there may be a return journey at lunch-time, and a second round trip in the afternoon — though these may 'turn short' and cover part of the route only. Where the distance is relatively short (up to ten or twelve miles, perhaps), there may be a more complex timetable, and on such routes we may still find there is enough demand for a service of some kind six days a week. A typical timetable might provide for a basic service on Mondays to Fridays, catering for commuters and school-children; extra journeys on market-day, and a midday return on early closing day; and two or three round trips on Saturdays. Such a service might require two buses on market-days and Saturdays, and one the rest of the week, leaving one of them free to run to another market town — perhaps a bigger place at a greater distance — on one of the other days.

A step up from this would be a service linking two towns, and catering for a

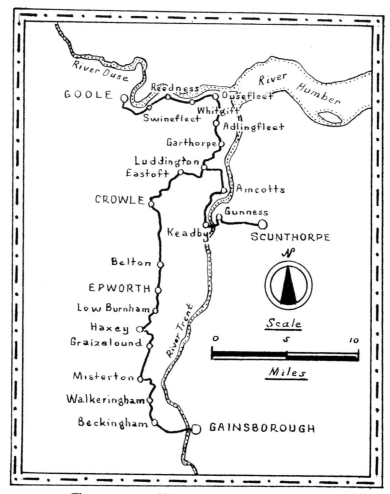

The two routes of Yorks & Lincs Motor Services

Buses and markets have always been linked, as here at Newton Abbot in very early days

certain amount of inter-urban traffic. Thus for many years the Yorks & Lincs Motor Service ran between Goole and Scunthorpe, being chiefly engaged in providing a service to one or other end of the route for the string of villages along the banks of the Humber and the Trent. Few indeed must have been the folks who made the journey over its full length: despite its grandiose title, this was another example of the country bus. Only rarely do we find the country bus advertised as an attraction to sightseers — one such was the Hanslope Direct Bus Service, in Northamptonshire, which made much of its route through Salcey Forest on the timetable sheet. While visits to relatives, or to solicitors or the local office of the DHSS, might be a purpose of the trip, the prime function of the country bus is, and has always been for shopping.

In some cases, strangers are actively discouraged, even if they succeed in finding where the bus leaves from. Timetable collectors (of whom the present author was for many years a most enterprising example) will often get no response to repeated postal requests, and may be regarded with deep suspicion if they call at a rural operator's premises and ask for a leaflet. Some enthusiasts find this difficult to understand, for they expect businessmen to seek new customers, but it may well reflect — in addition to a countryman's doubts as to

The bus at the seaside. The Dennis 'Ace' of East Kent, seen here outside the 'King Ethelbert' at Reculver, some time in the 1930s, was generally known as the 'flying pig'

Another 'flying pig', this, contrary to the indicator, was taken at Polperro in the mid 1930s, as Pearce's bus backs on to the stand ready to return to Looe

the bona fides of any 'foreigner' — a deeply felt sense that the service is for local people only. Anyway, a little research may show that the service does not exactly carry out the journeys that are provided for on the licence, because why bother the people at the licensing office so long as they don't bother you?

Where there are additions to the basic pattern of service, they too take on the pattern of community life. Commuting to work by country bus is about as far from the life of the tube-train commuter as the imagination can take it, but there will be a different kind of passenger to those who take the bus to market. All the same, the girls going to work in shops or offices in the town will have their own subjects for gossip, while the schoolchildren struggle with their homework, or float paper darts (till the driver stops them). On such services, too, the afternoon journey may carry bundles of evening papers, for the village shops and delivery boys, and there will be a spare copy for the driver as a courtesy of the trade.

An important function of the country bus in many places remains the commuter traffic. Not long ago I stood in Stafford, watching two Happy Days coaches and one from Greatrex Coaches waiting in a bleak and depressing corner of the town, at the kerbside, to start the evening journey back to the villages, and I wondered again at the low status of the bus as a means of transport in the eyes of local authority councils and planners. Without the buses, and the carriers before them, market towns like Stafford would have lacked much of their prosperity. But the jealousy between town and country is neither new nor distinctively British!

There is still one aspect of the country bus that must be mentioned, that doesn't have so much to do with shopping, and that is the 'outing'. But before we look at the excursion business, there is an aspect of the trade that flourished for some years, and has now all but disappeared, which was once known as the 'picture bus'.

For a generation, townspeople took it for granted that the cinema offered entertainment on demand, and many people took advantage of the notice 'programme changed twice weekly'. With the greater prosperity of the villages after 1945 there was a demand for similar advantages, and since even the smallest market town would have at least one if not two picture palaces, operators soon began to cater for it. It was a steady demand, throughout the year, and it cost little to provide a bus from half a dozen villages into town for about a quarter to

seven and back again at half past ten. Sometimes it was worth running twice a week — say on Wednesday and Saturday — to allow for the change of programme, and some operators ran one or more picture buses from different villages every weekday evening. For the driver it meant 10s (50p) in overtime, and for the proprietor it was a little jam on the bread and butter, assuming the bus had already earned its keep during the day.

Not all of the passengers patronised the cinema, for the picture bus left town at about the time the pubs closed, but the combination of mains electricity and television put an end to a short-lived but important function of the bus. I call up even now the atmosphere in a crowded 29-seater as we pull off the stand at Old Market Place in Sudbury, bound for Ballingdon, Bulmer, Catley Cross, Wickham St Pauls and Gestingthorpe, at 10.30pm on a summer Saturday. It is a memory of being among friends, and it illustrates the function of the bus — or coach — in giving country people a means of entertainment, which must be quite as important in its way as its function in providing for the shopping.

We caught a glimpse of an outing when we discussed the charabanc, and even before that, as we saw, there were trips in hay-carts, pulled by horses or even steam traction engines, that broke the monotony of country life. Today, even though cars are more common in the villages than they are in the towns, the coach plays an important part in rural life, and many firms make sure that they have one or two vehicles that offer the standard of luxury expected of the trade. They will have quite a variety of uses.

One will be the outing from the village pub. (If the pub hosts a darts club, there may be two such outings in the season.) With a certain amount of bottled beer in the boot, and chalk marks on one of the tyres for a little quiet gambling, turning upon which one comes up at the top when the party reaches its destination, this may seem an unpromising sort of trip, but the function of the pub outing is in part to provide a day out for the wives and children of the men who patronise the local, and rowdy behaviour is therefore not to be encouraged. Often the contract goes to the firm whose men use the pub when they are off duty, and individual drivers may be requested for the work. As with all such outings, the satisfaction of the party will be measured by the size of the driver's tip (sometimes irreverently called the 'dropsy'), which will come from a collection taken up on the way home.

For some years before and after World War II, country bus operators could add to their trade by contracting to take soccer, darts and cricket teams to away matches, and the custom was for the club to provide a list of fixtures, which were then priced at a flat rate irrespective of distance (in Suffolk this was known as quoting 'longs and shorts'). Today the car carries much of this traffic, but the club will still hire a coach for its outing, and probably there will be fewer wives and girlfriends and more drinking, calling for further professional skills on the part of the driver in getting everyone home. Southend or Blackpool illuminations have long been popular destinations, involving a late return — the family

A South Wales idyll, as the bus climbs out of the valley on a summer day on its way to Trinant

outing to the seaside will mean leaving for home no later than six o'clock. Sometimes though the outing will be to a pantomime or an ice show, with perhaps a free ticket for the driver, too.

Other bookings will have more of a rural purpose. The annual Fatstock Show is an attraction for farmers, while many coach parties are made up for the agricultural shows — both the local County Show and the Royal at Stoneleigh Abbey can be expected to provide work for the country operators. Most of the showgrounds now have adequate hardstanding for visiting coaches, but there have been times in the past when wet weather has prevailed, and coach parks have become quagmires, with the mud well distributed over the interior of the vehicles by returning passengers, and a heavy cleaning job for the driver next day.

Other sources of business will be churches and chapels, and the local Women's Institutes. In some villages there will be an 'organiser' — usually but not always female — who arranges coach trips, hiring the vehicle from the local firm, and selling seats. (This has for years been illegal, but virtually impossible to prevent.) Outings will be to the seaside in summer, and the pantomime in winter, with perhaps a shopping trip to the nearest city a few weeks before Christmas. It is difficult, and probably pointless, to distinguish this kind of thing from public excursions advertised by the operator, for what matters is the satisfaction that the passengers obtain. It would be very unwise to neglect the importance of the coach outing in thinking of the place of the country bus.

Let us conclude this chapter by returning to the vehicles themselves. It is perhaps impossible to describe a typical fleet, but we have seen that the average size is around five vehicles. Much will then depend upon how much stage carriage work is done, for the effect of the 'new bus grant' has been to add more specialised vehicles to many country fleets, with questionable results in terms of comfort. If then there are one or two more or less inter-urban services, we may expect to find some rather austere vehicles, whose hard seats with low backs to them indicate that they are truly buses.

As well as these, there will be coaches, and for many country firms, coaches will comprise all the fleet. They may well be Bedfords with bodywork that begins to look out of date, for we find here a phenomenon that the railways call the 'cascade effect', as vehicles that were new with one operator are sold down the market, finishing with the small firm that cannot afford to buy new, or even nearly new. All the same, there will be at least one firm in a given area that will have a better class of coach, and a 'connection' with a better class of customer as well. (Such a firm will almost certainly have good deal of private hire work arising in one or more of the nearer towns.) Some of the bigger firms may be predominantly coach operators, but even they may run a few small local services, keeping perhaps one or two older buses for the purpose.

The distinction between them all will lie in the livery — the vital means of recognising your bus or your coach, whether it is in the bus station at the market town, or the coach park at the seaside. The really down-market firm will not bother greatly, and may run vehicles with several different liveries, not having troubled to repaint them after buying them second-hand. This, though, is not well regarded in the trade, and we may run our eyes over the buses and coaches that we see, and recognise quickly just how professional is their owner. One driver said to me once, with respect to a rival operator: 'He keeps his coaches well, like the old farmers kept their horses.' Tradition dies hard in the country!

Southdown

7   Working on the Buses

There used to be a television series about a road haulage business, called *The Brothers*. Excellent entertainment that it was, it told us little about road haulage, but that may have been because goods are inherently less interesting than people. Now, a country bus firm would be quite a different proposition . . .

Once again, though, we must start with the difference between the big, town-based firms, and those whose business is really an integral part of the community that they serve. To begin with, they tend to attract different kinds of people to work for them, for some like the security of roster duties, the status of a uniform provided by the firm (as well as its economic advantage), and perhaps a certain anonymity, while others prefer the less predictable mixture of different kinds of work that they can expect in a smaller size of business. If you know the bus industry, you will recognise each type, and no doubt there is room for both, but the latter is the more likely to be found on the country bus.

In the years of expansion after World War I, road transport attracted many people away from agricultural trades — I once worked as a conductor to a man who had for years driven a steam traction engine, when only the steamers could provide enough power to plough the heavy Hertfordshire loam.[1] In the 1930s, when good Essex wheat land was changing hands for a few shillings an acre, the buses offered steady employment, while from the 1950s on the spread of new technology drove men off the land. Men who made such a shift were unlikely to move again, and the continuity of employment gave the small country bus firm its special place — as it still to a large extent continues to do. As seen in chapter six, the driver is part of the community of passengers on the village bus.

If he works from a village depot, he will of course be part of the village community too, and the passengers will know who his father and mother and uncles and aunts all are — for there has never been much privacy in village life. (In some parts of the country the social division is between 'residents' and 'villagers' — Kelly's Directories always listed the residents in each parish, who accounted for only a small part of the population — and residents have seldom used the country bus.) Because the job requires a certain self-reliance, and carries a degree of status too, some of the drivers may be 'characters', just as many country railwaymen used to be. Where women have worked as conductors they have often acquired an even more respected position, for the conductress is in a position to know a great deal about people's comings and goings.

---

1 The traction engines worked in pairs, pulling the multi-shared plough backwards and forwards on a wire cable — the plough had two sets of shares, so that it could work in either direction, and a man sat on a board at one end or the other, to weigh it down. When the lie of the land prevented the engine drivers from seeing each other, they used a system of smoke signals to indicate when to reverse the drive, and fetch the plough back the other way.

Some of the pioneers had a great sense of style, as in the case of P. Owen & Sons of Abberley, who owned this Maudslay in 1914. The picture was taken in Worcester, and shows the need to provide for parcels – on the roof

Not everything that drivers do is directly related to their work. There may be errands undertaken in the town on behalf of friends or relatives, or for a small consideration, perhaps in kind. Someone who visits the market town regularly, with a bit of time to spare, can become part of the trading community, and not all of the goods in the boot may belong to the passengers. Drivers whose work involves a late evening run back to the depot empty have been known to keep a shot-gun in the boot, with a view to picking up a few rabbits; some who have a garden or allotment may take a certain amount of produce to be disposed of on a market stall, by arrangement with the stallholder.

When the firm is larger, such practices are not so easy, for drivers cannot be certain to be on the same journeys each week. Larger firms tend to distrust the system whereby a driver has his own route, though drivers in the country are usually reliable over the takings — indeed, the passengers may well notice if there is anything amiss. There is no need for an inspector in such a business, whose members are linked more by tradition and mutual respect than by con-tract. It may well be difficult to distinguish the proprietor from the men, for the social life of the countryside tends to level out differences of wealth and status — save for the special position of the residents, of whose number the proprietor is unlikely to be one.

We shall see in chapter nine that even the family business may come to need an inspector, if it expands beyond a certain point. Perhaps that is why so many country bus firms remain small — certainly there is a problem if dishonesty has become serious enough to pay the inspector's salary out of the savings he can make. The function of an inspector in giving information to the public, on the other hand, can quite well be done by drivers and conductors, and there is one sizeable company in the Midlands today which has dispensed with inspectors altogether.

The expectations placed upon the bus crew may be considerable. There is the responsibility for the boot and its contents, and there is the need to help elderly passengers on and off the bus; to hand down bags and parcels; and maybe to hold a toddler while his mother gets off and opens the folding pushchair. A conductor who fails in these duties will not be popular, and firms that still employ conductors — of either sex — are thereby providing part of the service that the passengers expect to pay for. In our 'home' village, near Sudbury, there was a market bus on Thursdays that made twelve stops in the half mile of the village street, so that no one had far to walk home. Each time it was a ritual of farewells and helping with parcels and pushchairs, and in one case the conductor was expected to help an old lady down (she always had the seat inside the door); to carry her shopping bag, and walk with her up to the path to her door; to find the key under the mat, unlock the door, and let her in. Then she would wave from the door, and you could go back to the bus.

Strange things can happen, too. One driver I knew had an owl fly into the destination indicator of a double-decker he was driving at night, with enough force to break the glass (and fatal consequences for the unfortunate bird). Another told me how he had a hare run out from the hedge, and continue for a good while running in front of the bus (this would have been in the days before there was much motor traffic about). Eventually it ran off into a cottage garden — straight up the path, and into the open front door. The driver got out and told the cottager — who was digging at the side of the house, and had not seen the hare — and received the characteristically laconic response of a countryman: 'Well, 'e 'ont come out agin.'

Working hours and conditions on the country buses may seem easy in comparison with those of the urban industrial worker. As we have seen, there are two kinds of bus driver: the ones who like a predictable experience, so that they can see from the rota exactly which duty they will be on six weeks hence, and when their rest-days fall; and the ones who take the rough with the smooth, and are content to wait until the daily orders go up to see what they are doing tomorrow. (This of course does not mean that a specific rest-day cannot be negotiated for a particular purpose when required.) I doubt whether either type would be happy in the wrong sort of employment, but the former is more likely to find work with the big company than with the typical country bus proprietor. (He may still live in the village, and drive in each day to the depot in the town.)

The trade unions reluctantly recognise the distinction, and the national agreements on hours and conditions of work apply, by and large, to the big companies and not the small. The 'coaching trade' is seen to be a different industry, and most country bus firms are accepted as belonging to it. In practice, the national agreement would be quite unsuitable for these smaller firms, which depend upon flexibility, yet the normal working of the labour market sees to it that take-home pay is much the same in both cases. In some parts of the country there are associations of coach proprietors (many of them being the rural bus operators we are thinking of) that have reached agreements with the Transport & General Workers Union, but the ACAS report on the subject recognises that there is less desire for union membership and a greater individualism among coach drivers than there is in the urban and inter-urban bus industry. That conclusion goes for the country busmen, too.

In many firms the basic activity is the contract with the county council to carry schoolchildren. That this provision is sacrosanct was shown a few years ago, when the House of Lords refused to accept a government proposal to modify it. The driver's day may well turn upon the morning and afternoon school contract, when he will have what may be the doubtful pleasure of conveying junior or secondary schoolchildren from a number of villages, hamlets or isolated farms to a school which may be in the nearest town or may just as well be in one of the larger villages. (I say 'doubtful' because there are problems of discipline — or the lack of it — that might seem outside the normal responsibility of the driver — imagine driving an old-style double-decker with an open platform, and no adult on the back to keep an eye on the kids.)

If it is market-day the bus will be wanted back, and the driver will be on stage work until it is time to go back to the school for the return journey. If it is a quiet day, with no other work for the bus, then he will be 'on shops', or 'in the yard'; he will bring the bus back and change into overalls. If he has any craft or mechanical skills he will be kept busy with routine maintenance, and if not there will always be buses to wash, or perhaps steam-cleaning for a vehicle inspection, or maybe some painting and repair jobs on the premises themselves. The seats need to be thoroughly cleaned from time to time — luggage racks and other inaccessible places accumulate all kinds of rubbish, while there are various occasional things to be done such as easing a door that tends to jam, or renewing worn floor-covering. All this will be additional to the routine sweeping out and tidying up that is the driver's task at the end of each day's duty.

Sometimes a firm will have four or five coaches working contracts to the same school, and it may be economical to leave all but one of them there, and use that one to bring all the drivers back to the yard. There, under the direction of the guv'nor, and working with him and the full-time fitter, they may carry out heavier engineering work, especially in the quieter winter months. At Corona we reconditioned the engine of one of the two Leyland Tiger PS1/1 coaches, only using outside contractors for the rebore. Another way in which the school contracts may be covered when there is not much other work for the bus is to

90

employ part-time drivers, without whom many country bus firms could never carry on at all.

Part-time drivers are also used at weekends, and when regular staff are on holiday. The trade seems to attract some people — I had one man, a farmer, whose father had sold the family bus business, but who missed it so much that he would take a week's holiday between the hay and the harvest, when farming is quiet, and drive for me. He was invaluable because he only wanted to drive on the local services, or on London, where he had no objection to covering the 11.15pm down journey on a Saturday night, not one of the more popular duties. Another man kept a pub, and had a yard at the back where one of our coaches was stabled from Monday to Friday. He would take workmen to a factory some ten miles away, and then bring schoolchildren back. After a trip to the depot to fill up and sweep out he would take the bus home and cover the lunch-time pub trade, and then do the reverse of the morning trip before getting back for opening time. On Saturdays and Sundays the coach would be back at the depot for another part-timer or one of the regular men to drive.

Country bus conductors have tended even more to be part-timers. Some of them would be drivers' wives, but very often a service would only need a forward control vehicle twice a week, so that a driver working a 29-seater 'd/c' could cover the work on other days. Then a local lady would be employed on a 'regular part-time' basis, to conduct on market-day and Saturday. No doubt the opportunity to do the week's shopping without having to find the bus fare is a perk of the job, but demand for part-time conductors has never been all that strong, and so the conductress has never been without a certain status in the community. Some firms, though, have tended to use drivers in between contract work, while those with a regular daily service have employed full-time staff for the conducting function.

As for the tickets themselves, that is a whole specialism, and bus tickets attract a class of enthusiast collectors, many of whom are as distinguished as those Oxford dons of an earlier generation who made a hobby of collecting railway tickets. The student of the bus industry may indeed learn a good deal from the appropriate pages of the Transport Ticket Society's Newsletter. (Perhaps an apology is in order to Oxford dons of the present generation, who may collect railway, and even bus tickets; it is indeed a fascinating hobby.)

The earliest operators would have used the Bell Punch, if they used any ticket system at all, and it is still to be found in some remote places today. In its heyday the longer stage carriage services required long double-banked ticket racks for all the possible stages, even though some of the tickets were seldom called for. The tickets themselves sometimes carried nothing but the fare and the firm's name, but the full 'geographical' tickets would list all the fare stages, the idea being that a hole was punched against the one where the passenger intended to get off. These were expensive to produce, so the ticket printers invented what the collectors call 'deaf and dumb' tickets, which just had stage numbers printed down the sides. Either way there would be a range of colours for the various values, with separate series for singles and returns — the making of a collecting hobby almost as promising as stamps. Yet I never heard of a bus-ticket catalogue from Stanley Gibbons.

Punching a ticket in the exact spot is not really very easy, especially if you are doing it in a moving bus, after dark. I think it was a custom always more honoured in the breach than in the observance. In addition, the ticket that carries a price is an item of value, and the larger firms realised that the cost of ticket audit was considerable. To satisfy their needs, various other ticket systems have been developed, and most of them have been used by country bus operators in one place or another. One such was the Willebrew, which had all the potential fares printed down the side, and the conductor cut off a slice (which stayed in his punch), leaving the effective fare as the lowest one still showing on the ticket. This also required a certain dexterity, and some firms preferred the machines where the fare is written in pencil on the ticket, whereupon a lever ejects it from the machine, to be torn off and given to the passenger, while a carbon copy is kept inside.

Increasingly the large firms have progressed from this to some form of mechanical ticket-issue that keeps a record of its own. These machines print the ticket value and other information (such as stage numbers) on to either plain paper or paper that has the company's name (with perhaps an advertisement) on it already. For a long time the data capture has been through reading the counters on the machine, and this has meant the loss of a good deal of information that a Bell Punch waybill could provide to a skilled interpreter. For example, if you knew what the fares were for the principal stages on a route, the entries for each value and each journey on the waybill — itself a complicated document — could tell you a lot about how many passengers got on or off, where, and when. Today the big bus companies are using fully computerised ticket systems, which provide management with all the information that the Bell Punch did, and more — but it is open to question how far the small firm needs all this, anyway.

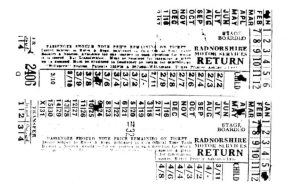

The *Willebrew* ticket

The Bell Punch became almost a cultural artefact, being copied in simple form in thousands of children's 'bus conductor' sets (seldom to be seen in the age of Action Man toys). Its great virtue was its simplicity, and the fact that it provided a numerical counter. It was also remarkably cheap — even the cost of the tickets could be offset by selling the space on the back to local firms for advertising. In small firms, too, the problem of audit was less serious, but as the larger companies gave it up, so it tended to be overtaken by newer, and usually more complicated systems.

The Willebrew was never popular with staff, because it was only too easy to cut off too little or too much if the bus happened to be going over a bump in the road, and then there would be problems in reconciling the waybill with the cash taken on the duty. Many of the ticket machines of the past forty years have been designed with the urban bus in mind, and have been incapable of providing for a long range of prices. For a good while the typical rural or inter-urban bus conductor, at least in the medium and large undertakings, would have been equipped with the product of the Setright works in east London, which was well suited to the type of work.

There were two types of Setright machine. Both incorporated a set of printing heads, which were selected by turning knobs on the side of the machine, and which were self-inking. These enabled a ticket to be endorsed with the fare paid, and other necessary information, including the fare stage, and the printing was done by turning a handle — to do this, you had to simultaneously release a finger catch, and let it back, so that the handle could only go round once; like so many things, this required a certain knack. The normal Setright printed the fare and the stage, and perhaps an 'S' or 'R', for single or return, together with the number of the machine, on a narrow roll of paper fixed to a spindle inside it, and when the handle was turned the 'ticket' was ejected, and had to be torn off to give it to the passenger. The 'insert' Setright, on the other hand, had a slot into which a card ticket was put, and the machine then printed the stage number and fare, etc, on to the end of it. (This was the sort of machine we shall meet in chapter twelve.) In either case, it will be plain, the actual ticket has no value until it has received the imprint of the machine, thus virtually removing the problem of audit.

Setright machines needed oiling, at infrequent intervals, and inking rather more often. The latter was a messy procedure, and most large firms employed fitters trained at the works to look after the stock of machines. It was always possible to rent them, too, but the really small firms never found them a worthwhile investment, tending to hang on to the Bell Punch. An alternative was a machine that is still to be found on London Transport, where the fare is set by a device rather like a telephone dial, and the ticket roll consists of thin paper — the imprint includes the name of the firm and other matter (such as the legal warning that it is issued subject to the company's regulations, etc), which is pre-printed on Bell Punch and Setright tickets. Machines of this kind, though, give very little traffic information, and serve only to act as a check on the cash to be paid in.

With the disappearance of the conductor has gone the practice of 'slinging a bag and punch' — the cash bag over one shoulder and the harness of the ticket punch over the other. Now the machine is fixed to some sort of stanchion at the driver's side, and the money goes into a kind of coffin — and heaven help us if we have not the right change! I am not at all sure that all this has been a change for the better, for it will not do if bus companies make it harder to use their services, and a simple ticket system may be all that is required.

What matters is a record of tickets sold, to match (hopefully) the cash collected, and a breakdown by journey. I know of at least one small firm that does very well with cloakroom tickets of different colours: there are only four or five stages, so each colour can represent a different fare. All that is necessary is to make a note of the number on the first unsold 'ticket' at the end of each journey, and the necessary financial and statistical information is there on record. Such a system is of course entirely dependent upon the honesty of the staff, but that is a commodity still more frequently found in the country than the town — and anyway, the guv'nor drives the bus himself often enough to spot any unusual factors. Errors do of course arise, and cash may be over or under the

Whenever we'm ahead o' time, them lot holds us up!

record of the tickets, but the common practice here is to require the correct money, leaving the conductor to make up 'unders' from the occasional 'overs'.

Making up the waybill can take some time, but there is usually spare time during the day. It can be done on the bus after arrival in town, or during a 'layover' out in the villages. Sometimes layover time has an unexpected social value, if we consider what happens to the driver, and perhaps the conductor, if there is one, while the bus stands idle for half an hour before returning to the town. Watch them as they leave it, and you may see them knock on the door and go into a nearby cottage, where an elderly couple are happy to make them a cup of tea, in return for their company; for perhaps a prescription filled on their behalf at the chemist's on the next trip; and especially for the knowledge that someone comes in regularly, and will be available to help in an emergency. It is in ways like this — seldom widely known — that the country bus becomes part of the community it serves.

In few of these firms will the drivers expect a uniform. Caps may be bought, and sometimes a white coat for the summer seaside excursions, but these are matters for the individual. The real means of identification will be the badge that comes with the public service vehicle driver's licence, which is made so that it can be worn in the buttonhole. (There used to be a similar badge and licence for the conductor, but these were done away with by the Transport Act of 1980.) At one time the possession of a badge was reckoned to ensure a free ride on a London Transport bus, through the unofficial freemasonry of the trade, but I have never been able to discover how far this was true in other cities.

Neither is there any very strong sense of rank among country busmen, beyond the normal superiority of long service. Sometimes one of the older men may acquire a sort of courtesy title as 'senior driver', but it will carry no extra pay, and its responsibilities will be the undefined functions of leadership as and when there may be a call for them. If the firm is unionised, the shop steward will have his own position, but he will be expected to earn it, and will find it hard to take advantage of it. In my own experience, I found that the shop steward and I worked very well together, but then I made a point of earning his confidence, and consulting him on any serious matters, like the introduction of a new ticket system, or major changes in the timetables and crew duties.

The one area in which seniority can play a part, though, is the share-out of private hire work. Whoever it is that prepares the daily orders must give careful thought to the allocation of drivers to both private outings and advertised excursions. Not only are these seen to be less demanding than stage carriage duties, but there is the matter of the 'dropsy'. This is such a recognised source of income that the Inland Revenue assumes it, and the sensible driver will declare a reasonable income from tips, because if he does not, the Revenue will impute a figure that it will then be up to him to disprove . Even so, tips represent cash in the hand, and some parties can be much more generous than others. Not for busmen is the catering practice of pooling tips and sharing them out; each retains his own. And this means that it can be worthwhile to set a sprat to catch a mackerel, so that some drivers I have known have bought newspapers and magazines and put them out on the seats before picking up a private party. No doubt their reward was the greater.

As we have seen, some customers specify the driver they require, while some drivers may simply not be suitable for certain types of customer. Happy the firm whose traffic manager can balance out the conflicts that arise, allowing for the need to respect drivers' hours regulations, and at the same time leave no one feeling hard done by! Above all, the plum jobs must not be given to part-timers — and neither must the guv'nor drive too many of them himself.

The season for outings is predictable. From late May to the end of the school term there will be good work to be had, with various social clubs and Women's Institutes to the fore. The small firm may find a strain here, if some of its coaches are still tied up with school contracts. There will be a certain amount of Saturday work, but since Saturday is a shopping day, this may be less than there is on offer during the week. Firms with a good 'connection' may pick up more exacting work, for organisations like County Archaeological Societies, and this is a time when it may be possible to fill a few more imaginative excursions on Sundays (ensuring that the drivers know their way, for some may be reliable only for places they know how to find). With the school holidays there are more coaches available, and the seaside trip comes into its own, though at a half or two-thirds of the adult fare, the extra children on an excursion can soon take the shine off its profits.

But summer Saturdays are a slack time for coach hire, and few firms offer excursions. Again this is due partly to people's shopping habits, but Saturday is also the day to start or finish a holiday. For many years the smaller businesses have found work on Saturdays by sending coaches on hire to those firms that provide holiday express services. Since the 1930s these services have been consolidated in the ownership of the territorial bus companies, most of which developed a coaching side to their business, and these finally came into state ownership between 1949 and 1969. A few remained in private hands, though, and a good many private businesses developed seasonal holiday services after 1945. None of them could afford to maintain a fleet large enough to cope with the peak summer Saturday demand, and so it became essential for them to use hired coaches, which the smaller firms were very happy to supply. Thus a driver may find himself on the local market service on Friday, and the next day driving 'on hire' to National Express from Torquay to Victoria Coach Station, in London.

Now let us see what some of these journeys are like for the people who work on the buses. First let us take a conductor, working for a medium-sized country bus firm in the 1950s — it is a winter morning, and the duty commences at 6.30am. Having overcome the first hurdle, and got our elderly, pre-war car to start, we

96

The Golden Age of Buses, when there was so little traffic in Brentwood High Street that Curtis's Ongar & District Chevrolet could pull away onto an empty carriageway. Beside it is a Reo belonging to F. H. Nugus, waiting to leave for Herongate, while further back there is an Eastern National Gilford, formerly one of Edward Hillman's Bluebird saloons

make our way through mist and thinning darkness to the depot, situated on the outskirts of a village that is twelve miles from the nearest town. Drivers and fitters are starting buses of all kinds, for the fleet is a mixed one, several smaller firms having been combined to make the one we work for. With the car parked out of the way, we enter the rest-room, a Nissen hut that doubles as a paying-in office, and collect a ticket machine, a cash bag and a float of change — one pound, in silver and coppers. No one says much — it is too cold, and everyone seems to be sleep-walking as we cross the yard amidst clouds of vapour from exhausts, where the buses are being warmed up.

Ernie, our driver, is a big man with a country accent, wearing a brown overall coat. We have a double-decker, second-hand from London Transport, that has certainly seen better days, and as Ernie pulls out on to the lane we go and sit up at the front, to get away from the draught sucked in at the open back platform. Moving quickly in a snow storm, this can make the rear half of the lower saloon uninhabitable, but this morning the sun is rising to a clear sky. Several of the other buses will have started picking up as soon as they left the depot, but we are running 'dead' (not 'light', as in railway parlance) to take up the first journey from the nearest town into a larger one, fifteen miles away. This means we have time to enter the opening numbers from the ticket machine on to the waybill, though the cold makes it difficult to write plainly.

When we pull on to the stand, a hardy few are waiting, and we know them all. A few more hail us as we leave the town, and then we stop here and there in the lanes — it is surprising where people come from, for sometimes there will be a passenger waiting at a corner with not a house in sight. The work is easy as yet, for there is no rush as the bus fills up gradually, and the trips upstairs begin to stir the blood in our veins. By the time we reach our last picking-up point, for we are not allowed to carry local traffic within the town we are going to, the bus is full, though, and it is a bit of a challenge to get every fare in, and cancel every weekly ticket that is presented to us. But it is full daylight now, and a busload of passengers generates a good deal of warmth. (If it is a Monday, with all those weeklies to issue, then we shall be really ready for a coffee at the bus station, before we set out to do another round trip before 9am.)

For our second example, let us take a driver employed by a rather smaller firm, and this time it is late May, early in the 1960s. This time we face that unpopular duty, a 'split shift'. The running sheds are in the village, and we can cycle to work, and we shall not need any tickets this morning, because we are on contracts. The first journey leaves from the garage, and there are one or two people waiting for us already, as we start the 33-seater Bedford with its Duple Vega body — really rather a superior bus for workmen, but that is what it said on the duty board. There is something pleasant about being around early on a spring morning, and most of the passengers will be familiar. If anyone is missing, we wait and hoot, unless maybe someone else can tell us he is not coming today. Having started at ten past seven, we are at the factory for ten to eight, as per schedule, and away again, this time running dead.

It is a fairly tight timing, for we have to get to a village six miles away to start a school run back to our nearest town. These will be secondary schoolchildren, going to the boys' grammar and the girls' high schools, amd most of them will still be doing their homework. We meet two of our mates, driving the other way with children for the secondary modern school that we have passed, and they have clearly got a livelier load! By a quarter to nine we have said goodbye to our lot, and there's time for a coffee, so we pull up on one of the vacant stands in the market place.

Here there will be other drivers, and conductors, from our own firm and others. Some of them will be away again at nine o'clock, but the rest of us will congregate in the milk bar, over coffee and jokes with the counter girls. How pleasant to be taking things easy, when others have all started work! But we don't hang about long — it is time to take the coach back to the depot.

We are off duty now, until two-thirty, which means time for gardening. Bread and cheese and a bottle of beer, and back to the running shed in good time to pick up a bag and punch, and take out a 29-seater, another Bedford, but this time with bodywork by Thurgood of Ware — very like a standard Vista, but built with heavier timbers. It is market-day, and the local service needs to be strengthened, so we are — according to the duty board — on the 'dishy bus'; no reference to its glamour, but slang for 'additional'. There is no timetable to keep to, because we are what is also called a 'floater', and our job is to relieve the buses coming in from a longer distance of the local traffic over the busy last four or five miles in and out of town. It is known that one of our competitors over this section employs a part-timer for this work, on the basis that the contents of the bag are evenly divided at the end of the afternoon.

By half past four the traffic is slackening, so we make one last trip out of town, and then carry on to the depot, where we pay in. There is just time to slip home for tea, and then we sweep out the coach and at six we are outside the village pub, for the Women's Institute are going to a meeting in the county town, twenty miles away. We would rather have been taking the darts team, but it's 'swings and roundabouts', and there will be time for a pint while they are at the meeting; at least they won't be late home.

Neither shall we, and at ten o'clock we are back in the yard. The coach must be swept out again — no one leaves that job for another man to do in the morning — and the petrol tank must be filled and the oil checked. It has been a long day, but isn't it better than being tied to a lathe from eight till five, like the chaps we took to work this morning?

8 Coaching Interlude

Petrol engines are not so common now, though for a long time there were coach proprietors who regarded them as preferable to diesel. Bedford and Ford both sold petrol-driven coaches in large numbers, long after the ubiquitous Gardner diesels had shown the reliability of the compression-ignition engine. We shall return to the subject in the next chapter, but the choice of engine has always been important for the coaching trade, and for some of the larger country bus firms the mileage expected of their coaches justifies the higher cost of the diesel, and its greater complexity. Any good motor mechanic can maintain a petrol engine, but trained diesel fitters are not so easy to come by, as seen in chapter five.

Coaching for the small firm is largely a matter of catering for day trips to the seaside, or to the nearest town or city, for shopping, football or the pantomime, no matter whether the trip is organised by a customer or advertised by the firm as a public excursion. This is a part of country transport that is much older than the bus, and its social value is much greater than might be thought. It is easy to feel superior about the 'bingo bus' that relieves the monotony of life by taking people to the town one evening a week, but for those who use it, its importance may be as great as that of the weekly market bus. (Despite this, the fuel tax will be rebated for the market bus, and probably won't be for the bingo trip!)

Firms of this kind will traditionally have had a fleet of coaches, at least since the charabancs were replaced by all-weather saloons. They will use them to provide their market bus services, but it is obviously easier to use a coach on a bus service than the other way round. The diesel engine has been slow to make its mark in this type of business, but there have always been some firms with wider horizons, who have shared with the town-based subsidiaries of the 'combine' the responsibility for the express coach services.

The first true long-distance coach service was started on 11 February 1925, between Bristol and London. Previous services had been little more than seaside excursions, usually carrying people only between the terminal points, but the Greyhound coaches had single and return fares between all the stage points, and they ran daily throughout the year. Within five years a network had grown up that covered most of England and Wales (but never really penetrated into Scotland until quite recently), and many small firms took part in its development. Then, after 1931, the combine companies bought most of these small businesses (they too were usually town-based), and thus was formed the network now operated by National Express.

Quite soon, though, the coaches in some parts of the country began to find a role in serving the villages they passed through. All over the Westcountry in the

1930s the Royal Blue became a household name for travel, which even its acquisition by the partly railway-owned Southern and Western National Omnibus Companies did not discourage. While the services tended to follow the main roads, they were scheduled to call at the villages, and by the end of the decade the unmistakable beat of the Gardner five-cylinder diesel engine would herald the appearance of a Royal Blue Bristol coach, stopping outside the village shop that had the booking agency, to pick up or set down its passengers.

The standards of comfort of those coaches were if anything superior to the third-class railway carriages of the day, while the fares were half those of the trains. All the same, they were by no means a down-market form of transport — while the Saturday traffic in the summer was predominantly lower-middle-class families going on holiday, it was rumoured that you might share part of your journey with a titled lady, if you went in the middle of the week.

The decor of the inter-war luxury coach can still be seen in preserved vehicles of the period. Some firms stated that they ran 'parlour coaches', and the term is apt. Windows were fringed by neat curtains that were not usually meant to be drawn, and their full drop glass panes were controlled by crank handles which could be an uncomfortable protuberance if you found yourself on the inside seat, with a rather large neighbour. By the 1930s, moquette was beginning to re-place leather, and was usually carried throughout the trim, giving a cosy atmosphere, enhanced by the seat-backs, which were higher and more substantial than we are used to today.

The typical half-cab, forward control coach of the day, long and lean by comparison with the underfloor-engined vehicles of the past thirty years, would have a restrained external decor, often with an attempt to give the impression of streamlining — this was the period of the Silver Jubilee and Coronation stream-lined trains. The body side would often have a long flash, widening towards the rear, and turning downwards to reach the skirt aft of the back wheels. This replaced the more decorous panel of a contrasting colour along the waist, and gave the coach a rakish look. While some urban coach operators went in for elaborate scroll work, most country firms preferred a restrained version of the fleet name, though less austere than the usual style of the combine companies, with their first and last letters in capitals, and a heavy rule under the rest. (The Southdown vehicles always had a cursive fleet name, that gave them a less formal look than the buses of most other big firms.)

These coaches had springing that was much improved over the harsh ride that seems to have been characteristic of the charabancs. It has always been a criti-cism of the Ford product that their coaches were really lorry chassis, yet this was true also of the Bedford, and several other makes of the period, that never attracted the same reputation. They had without exception the cranked start-ing-handle that is lacking today from even the family saloon, but self-starters were coming in, sometimes confusing drivers unfamiliar with the new diesels, which required the use of a rather similar device to *stop* the engine. But the diesels were the mainstay of the territorial companies, and country operators hung on to petrol for many more years, even where they ran express coach services of their own.

Oddly enough, the rural coach service was to be found to a greater extent in the south and west than in other parts of England. In the Midlands the Midland 'Red' company developed a whole network of 'limited stop' bus services, the numbers carrying the 'X' prefix that warned passengers of a minimum point-to-point fare. These certainly performed a valuable social role, and since they did not require pre-booking, they could serve the villages with a minimum of formality. The mighty Crosville company, spanning the coast from Cardigan to Liverpool and reaching inland to the Pennines, had its inter-city coach services, but the villages in its territory were served by traditional buses until the post-war years. Ribble's Leyland Tigers purred up and down the A5, connecting London with Blackpool and the North West, but they were not in the business of serving intermediate towns and villages, while the other express coach services of the industrial north were largely inter-urban links, often of a limited-stop nature. Only in the far North did there develop two remarkable coach lines, spanning the country almost from sea to sea.

One of these, the GNE (Great North of England) took the A66 road across the Pennines, linking Darlington with Penrith, and extending certain journeys to Middlesbrough to the east and Keswick to the west. Between Bowes and Brough this is a high moorland road, but still further north the firm of Wright Brothers established their Newcastle–Alston–Penrith–Keswick service, based at Nenthead, the highest village in England. Keith Turns, who described the firm in his book *The Independent Bus,* tells us that Nenthead has 'three times the rainfall of Manchester and a climate approaching that of the Faroes. Nestling around the 1,500ft level, snow has been known in June, and is common in May.' As he says, the winter operation 'separates the men from the boys'. This is rural coach operation at its toughest, without even the railwayman's welcome sight of a semaphore to say the line ahead is clear.

Services like these grew up to link the countryside with the city, and nowhere were they more frequently to be found than in East Anglia and north Essex, where they were able successfully to compete with the London and North Eastern Railway. This was because the LNER lines had been built to run cross-country, between the two trunk routes from Liverpool Street to Norwich and King's Lynn. As a result the coach could offer a journey more nearly competitive in time to the train for passengers going to London from Bury St Edmunds and Braintree; Hadleigh and Haverhill; and the many smaller places in between. I had the experience of operating one such route, from Stowmarket (on the Norwich line) through the villages to Lavenham and then on through Sudbury, Halstead, Braintree and Chelmsford to arrive at King's Cross coach station four hours and twenty minutes later. At Sudbury, feeder coaches came in from Had-

The country coach service – Jennings and Premier Travel side by side at Kings Cross Coach Station on a Friday evening in 1963, waiting to take the travellers home

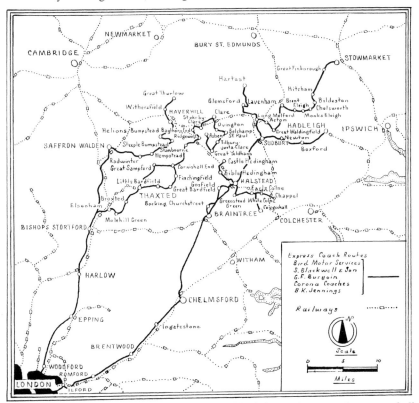

In Essex and Suffolk the express coaches in the 1930s filled the gap between the two main lines out of Liverpool Street

This must be a Sunday School treat – and good revenue for the owners of the 'all-weather saloons' (which replaced the charabanc) that brought the party to Southsea. The year is about 1929-30

There's an irresistible air of happiness about this very substantial outing by chara

leigh and Hartest (the service was no doubt responsible for the withdrawal of passenger services on the LNER Hadleigh branch in 1932).

From Stowmarket the train would obviously have got you to London more quickly, but from the villages the overall journey time would have been less attractive, and even from Lavenham (where there was a branch line), many train journeys meant two changes, and all of them meant one. So it was not just the lower fares that attracted people to the coach; there was a factor of convenience. Just as it had been in stage-coach days, the village had its own direct link with the big city (not to mention the smaller towns, for which the coach served also as an ordinary country bus). And there was one special attraction, for everyone knew the drivers — they had been on the service since it started, and they came from the villages it served. They were a reassurance that was lacking in the impersonality of the main-line train, and they actually took you all the way!

Most of these country coach services have become part of the National Express network now, and are worked by drivers from the towns. In a few places there have been new ones started, since the restrictions on obtaining a licence were removed in 1980, but they were at their strongest during the twenty years after 1929. Even when the Ministry of Transport made operators suspend the principal express coach network during World War II, the East Anglian operators were allowed to continue, using railheads at places like Chelmsford and Bishop's Stortford, and some of the Royal Blue services were replaced by limited-stop buses.

But still, the rural express coach service has always been unusual, and it was a singular lack of imagination that prevented British Railways from encouraging the development of the species as part of its closure programme in the 1960s. Lumbering Bristol double-deckers, rigidly following closed lines irrespective of the destinations people wanted to reach, were bound to disappear as soon as the railway subvention had been withdrawn. The mistake was at least as much the responsibility of the territorial bus companies, with whom the railways had been financially linked since the end of the 1920s. The country bus proprietor, with his detailed knowledge of local demand, was not seen as having the necessary reliability — or perhaps it was just that he spoke a different English. Where there was no 'sister company' the railway managers were forced to negotiate with the local independent, and they were not always at ease in doing so.

But then, bureaucrats like to speak to bureaucrats, and rural coach operation is basically a matter of carrying private parties, whose organisers are capable of pretty hard bargaining to get the rate they want. Trips to the seaside, shopping trips, coaches for dances at neighbouring village halls; all these are in the day's work, and — as we have seen — they are every bit as important to those who use them as are the scheduled bus and coach services. The Women's Institute wants to go to the county town for a rally; the parish priest has a party to go to a

pilgrim's shrine; the National Farmers' Union branch wants a coach to take men to the Smithfield Show. Schools have outings, and need coaches for them, and so do supporters who want to get to football matches — watch the roads from Wales and the marches to Manchester on a Saturday when United is playing at home; many of the seemingly endless stream of coaches will have come from the villages. (Only when there is an International at Cardiff will Rugby Union exert so strong a pull in North and Central Wales.)

If you want to find out the catchment area of a British city, go round the coach parks in the weeks before Christmas, and see where the coaches come from. People from the towns will have trains or regular coach services to use, but at this time of the year there is a regular demand from village people, wanting to do their Christmas shopping. From north Devon they go to Plymouth; from Herefordshire to Birmingham; from South Humberside to Leeds. These are coaches that are part of the life of the countryside, whose drivers will wait for everyone to be on board again before starting the journey home. And as like as not the coach will be on the market bus service the following day.

Many regular private hire customers have their own preference for one or another driver, and this must be remembered in allocating the work. The coach driver's job is a highly personal one, which may account for the relative lack of interest in trade union membership. It is a job that has always attracted what used to be called 'a better class of man' — the phrase is unfairly snobbish, but hard to avoid. There is responsibility for expensive equipment, but that is also true of the bus driver, who — in the towns at least — seems to be much less identified with his work. Express service work in particular may be relatively lonely, and drivers have something in common with the independence of mind of the long-distance lorry-driver — though in other ways they are very different. Perhaps there may still be something in Mr Tony Weller's words to his son, Sam, in *Pickwick:*

"Cos a coachman's a privileged indiwidual,' replied Mr Weller, looking fixedly at his son. "Cos a coachman may do vithout suspicion wot other men may not; 'cos a coachman may be on the wery amicablest terms with eighty mile of females, and yet nobody think that he ever means to marry any vun among them.'

At Llanarth, Cardiganshire, in 1907, a GWR Milnes-Daimler caters for private hire traffic in between working the New Quay–Llandyssul rail feeder service. Clearly an 'occasion' for the whole village

Close inspection reveals the presence of the parson in his dog-collar, so we may suspect that this is a choir outing – the passengers seem a bit old for a Sunday School treat. The charabanc was pictured in 1919, and was owned by Hornsbys, the north Lincolnshire operator

This is such a rarity it couldn't be left out – a Leyland Titanic belonging to an Essex bus operator and looking very much a coach, despite having started life as a 6-wheel double-decker

9 The Country Bus Business

Sometimes, glimpsed out of the corner of the eye as he passes, the car driver will recognise an operator's yard. Most people will think no more of it, but the enthusiast, or the professional busman — and there is a hidden enthusiast inside most busmen — will do a quick double-take. Whose coaches are *they*? Or, if the firm is familiar, the response will be 'Not much change there', or 'So he's got a new vehicle'. This time, though, we are going to stop and poke around.

Somehow the word 'depot' is hardly suited for what we shall find. It is big firms in towns that have depots — small firms, and especially country bus firms, have garages. 'Where is Bloggs's bus garage?' you might ask. Yet the word 'yard' is irresistible, too, for the buses will not always be kept under cover. The garage itself may have been big enough to house the two Model 'T' Fords that the proprietor's grandfather started the business with, but it is more likely now to be the repair and maintenance shed, with perhaps an inspection pit and some fairly basic equipment.

There can be no telling where we shall find the bus garage. It may be in the village street (much deplored by the better-off residents, for whom it spoils the amenities). There may be petrol pumps, dating from before the days of planning controls, with those swing arms that carry the hose across the pavement to the cars that stop at the kerb. The office may have a shop-front, with displays about seaside trips if it is the summer, or pantomimes in the winter; and perhaps blackboards fixed to the walls, with announcements according to season. If the firm runs a local service, its timetable *may* be displayed in a glass case on the wall, but you can't rely on it. The common assumption seems to be that the people who need it know when the bus goes anyway.

Penetrate the office and who can say what you will find? Perhaps the sort of neat, tidy, well-decorated surroundings you would expect of a small travel agent — which perhaps is what it is. But more probably not: the interior may even be depressingly run-down and untidy, almost like a TV set for a situation comedy. Such surroundings need be no indication of how efficiently the business is being run, though, for the gaffer may just be more interested in his buses than his premises. What you must expect, as a stranger, is a certain amount of suspicion. It will not amount to hostility, but the fact remains that you may be someone from the Ministry, or the Health and Safety inspectorate, and in this world the official is suspect. Perhaps the biggest difference between the country railway and the country bus is the absence of bureaucracy, and the independent spirit of operators and their staff, free as they are from any superiors up the line. Their main concern is to make money — few of them make a lot, but it's a living, and many of them seem to enjoy it.

The country bus at home. Pulham's Bedfords at his Gloucestershire depot – probably the late 1950s

Part of the fleet of Hart, who ran from Otterton to Exmouth, and favoured the Commer

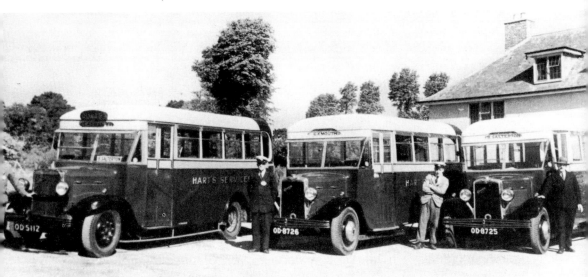

The office will be there to take bookings from customers for private hire, and to accept payment of their accounts; to see to the bare minimum of paperwork required for running the business and satisfying the auditors and the Traffic Commissioner; and for drivers to collect their ticket machines and pay in their takings, if local services are operated. The proprietor will probably spend as little time as possible there, and it may not even be open all the time. If the firm is big enough, though, it may employ a manager, and he will perhaps share the office with a typist, who will also deal with enquiries when he is out.

Lincolnshire carriers. The picture, taken at Grimsby in about 1925, includes Beasley of Immingham, Wilson of Binbrook, Stark of Tetley, Grantham of Ashby and Rook of Laceby. By this time they were all running motors (Source: PRW collection, original supplied by the Wilson family)

Strangers will be even more unwelcome in the garage itself. If it fronts on to the street there may be doors at the back, leading to an area of hardstanding, where the coaches are kept, or there may be a separate entrance to the yard. Here we can see for ourselves the make-up of the fleet.

Since the average size of bus fleets in Britain is less than five vehicles, we must not expect to see a lot — and anyway, they ought to be out, earning money. But private sector firms do very much less mileage than the big bus companies and municipal undertakings (while still making a living out of it), so if it is the middle of the day in school term, or a winter Sunday morning, the whole fleet may be there. If it is a weekday, there will be drivers about: someone will be hosing a coach down, another will be working with the fitter on one of the vehicles actually in the garage, while someone else is changing a tyre, or easing a sliding door. We shall not expect to find the latest high-floor super-coaches here — just the standard, box-like Ford or Bedford, or perhaps a Leyland. Many of them will be petrol driven, so that the emotive roar of a diesel being started up may not meet our ears. There are exceptions to all this, for some firms that are based in the country may be large enough to own the sophisticated coaches of the 1980s, but even so, most of *their* trade will come from the nearest towns, or even from international contracts, so that they are hardly typical of the country bus.

We walk across the yard, noting the livery. In recent years there has been a fashion for something more garish, with parallel stripes in bright colours that make sudden angular turns, far removed from the imitation streamlining of the

1930s. Fleet names appear in bold letters, designed to hit the eye. But there may not be so much of this where we are now, for country bus firms tend to be more conservative. The less professional ones may not even have a single livery, owning a few coaches bought second-hand and still in the colours of their former owners. Standards in this area have always varied, and it is equally true that some firms take a lot of trouble to keep a good public image in the way their coaches are painted, lettered, and kept clean.

But it is when we look at the back of the yard that we may see some signs of past glory. Large firms tend to sell vehicles to smaller ones, who resell them to others, and what the railways call the 'cascade effect' is an important part of the trade. The country bus proprietor, who is not likely to be among the wealthiest firms, is going to acquire a number of coaches that are approaching the end of their useful life, and these he may not be able to resell. They may indeed have reached the stage where the Certifying Officer — the ultimate 'man from the ministry' — refuses to allow them to be used any more on the public road. It is true that the standards required of small firms in the back of beyond are less rigorous than those applied to large firms with high annual mileage (this will be vigorously denied, but it is common knowledge all the same), but the standards are still very much higher than those that apply to the private car — or the average minibus. It is the least we expect of the public authorities, to ensure our safety when we travel by bus or coach.

But operators sometimes get attached to their vehicles, and are loath to scrap them — or so it seems from the range of de-licensed coaches and buses that we may find, in various stages of decay, at the back of the yard. For 'preservationists' this may be a happy hunting-ground, though the proprietor may not be keen to allow them in to look. It is when the garage lies well outside the village that there may be a better opportunity.

In such cases, though, whether the site is on a main road or at the end of a lane, the enquirer may be regarded with even more suspicion. There may well be no public office. An adjoining house may be the home of the owner, or of his manager, if the owner has moved a little bit up in the world, and left the roof his father provided when the business was first begun. Somewhere — either in the house, or even in a hut in the yard — there will be a traffic office of some kind, though, where essential records are kept, and pay-packets are made up each week. On the hardstanding there will be the usual mixed fleet of vehicles, and much the same activity will be going on. Firms that are situated like this will depend upon booking agents in the neighbouring villages and small towns for their trade, and while they may pay lower rates on their property, they would seem to be at a disadvantage. Yet there are many of them, and they seem to flourish in a quiet way.

It is not at all unusual for the country bus to be run by a multi-purpose business, in which the coaches play a greater or smaller part. If the garage is on the main road, then the filling station may be more substantial than it was in the example we have just looked at. Some car maintenance and repairs may be done, and a few country bus firms have retail agencies for cars, making a living out of an apparently competing mode of transport. Mixing goods and passenger services was once very common, but has been very much reduced over the past forty-five years. The days are long gone when goods and passenger bodies could be changed over, so that the same basic vehicle could carry goods and parcels on weekdays, and passengers at weekends. (Or perhaps they have not — the development of 'demountable' bodies for freight vehicles in recent years hints at interesting possibilities.)

Those who work in these firms may do various jobs, which is one of the things that makes the country bus so different from the rest of the industry. If there is a taxi business, the drivers will turn out in a cab as readily as a coach, and there is at least one rural coach operator that has branched out, so to speak, into undertaking. The days when a business could survive on public transport alone are not entirely gone, but the country bus proprietor is a businessman, who is going to seek his profits where they can be found. If there is a chance of paying the rates on the office by selling sweets and cigarettes, then he will take it. Sometimes the office is in the market town — even though the garage is out in one of the villages the buses serve — and then it may be worthwhile turning part of it into a café, or (as we saw) developing a travel agency business.

There are still routine jobs concerned with the buses. In all but the smallest firms there must be some form of ticket system, so as to ensure that takings are properly accounted for, and to provide some basic traffic information. As well as 'keeping the books' it will be someone's job to issue the equipment and the float of change, and to cash up the takings when the drivers come back. As well as the usual keeping of national insurance and PAYE records that would apply in any other business, there is the matter of drivers' hours, and not only is the law exceedingly complex, but records have to be kept for possible examination. Finally, coaches must be fitted with tachographs, which record the distance travelled, the stops made and the speeds achieved. The clerical side of the business can provide work for local people, both full-time and part-time, that is a useful part of the local economy; only in the very small firms do we find the old tradition of the proprietor's wife keeping the books on the kitchen table after tea. But then, that was more feasible in older days, when the formalities were much simpler.

Little has been recorded about the wife and family of the country bus proprietor, but one thing is certain: the job is not one that you can leave behind at the end of the day's work. Even twenty-five years after giving up my own business I still tend to jump when I hear a telephone, for too often that sound meant trouble. In a small business, especially, the public expect someone to be on call at more or less any time, and while drivers can usually deal with minor breakdowns themselves, if there is anything serious, then the guv'nor has got to go

Coach operators in the country may well have more than one string to their bow

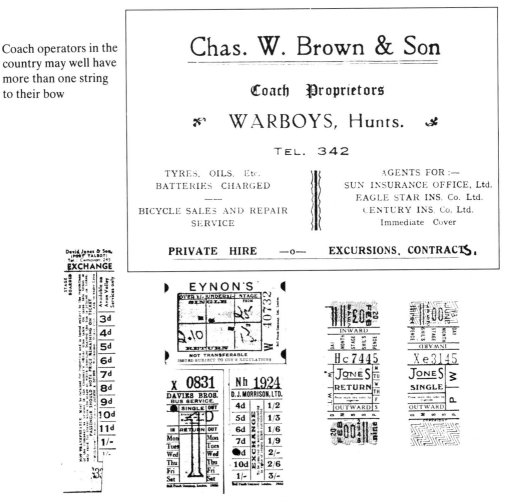

Chas. W. Brown & Son

Coach Proprietors

WARBOYS, Hunts.

TEL. 342

TYRES, OILS, Etc.
BATTERIES CHARGED
——
BICYCLE SALES AND REPAIR
SERVICE

AGENTS FOR :—
SUN INSURANCE OFFICE, Ltd.
EAGLE STAR INS. Co. Ltd.
CENTURY INS. Co. Ltd.
Immediate Cover

PRIVATE HIRE   —o—   EXCURSIONS, CONTRACTS,

A selection of bus tickets from South Wales independent operators

How to put the back of the ticket to good use

and deal with it himself. And that means leaving his wife to answer the phone.

On the other hand, there is usually enough leisure to pursue other interests. I have the clearest memory of one firm whose premises I used to visit but rarely, because the proprietor also bred whippets, and the smell of boiling bones permeated the running shed where he was generally to be found. In a trade so closely connected with the community it serves, the busman needs to have his links well forged with others around him, and however demanding the job may be, he cannot afford to be lost in it entirely. Above all, though, he must know his men.

What has changed least is the central part of every manager's day — 'doing the orders'. In large firms the drivers work to a rota, and all they have to be told is what changes there may be from day to day. In the smaller business there is less complication to deal with, but the drivers have got to be told what to do, and what bus to use. If there are just three or four market-day services the daily orders may say against each man's name no more than the destination and the number of the bus (the registration number, for fleet numbers are almost unknown in such firms). In term-time there will probably be a school contract, identified by the name of the school. If the day's work is a pub outing all that the orders may say is 'Black Boy to Clacton, 8.30am', with again the number of the coach — all the other details will be on the driver's work ticket. Where each driver keeps the same coach the orders may be simpler still, but in any case they are likely to be very informal, and in very small firms the instructions may actually be given by word of mouth.

This is the heart of the operation. Whoever is responsible for doing it is really the manager, and may well be a woman. At busy times the daily orders become a constant pre-occupation, and the allocation of men and machines for the next few days will be done mentally, or in rough, so as to be able to respond to uncertain or unexpected circumstances. Weather is always a complication, for the art of making money out of excursion traffic is to sell every seat. If you have filled one coach for Morecambe by Friday evening, what are the chances of filling another on Saturday? Much may depend upon the weather forecast, but if you 'let it run' and go on taking bookings, you may finish up with half a load on the second coach, and make a loss. On the other hand, if you 'stop booking' and phone the shopkeepers that act as booking agents, and the weather stays fine, you may have missed the chance of a profit. No wonder some firms prefer to stay in the business of providing coaches on hire to other people, who organise the trip and make the sales!

For many country firms there is the possibility of a telephone call from a larger neighbour, often a part of the National Express coach system, wanting to hire a coach and driver to duplicate one of their services. The law permits a firm to operate 'on hire' in this way, and while the work is not always very remunerative, it is certain money. As you plan the daily orders for the coming summer weekend, all these things will be in your mind. The drivers, too, have to be

114

considered, for they must not be allocated work that would lead them — and you — to offend against the complicated drivers' hours regulations that are laid down by bureaucrats in Brussels. And as well, the coach work involves tips, and so it must be equitably shared out.

No wonder the traffic side of the business, as all this is called, is enough to keep someone busy full-time in all but the smallest firms. The typical country bus proprietor in the past has probably been glad to leave it to a manager, whose title may be a slight exaggeration, since he or she will really be a sort of chief clerk, despite the responsibility of the job. For a business owning between ten and twenty vehicles there will be such a manager, with perhaps a person to keep

Vehicles and staff of J. T. Friskney of Horncastle in about 1933, a firm taken over by the Lincolnshire Road Car company shortly after this photo was taken. One of the buses is a Bedford WLB; another probably a Chevrolet (Source: PRW collection)

the books and see to the ticket-issue, and a girl to answer the phone and do a bit of typing. Traditionally, in many such businesses the proprietor has been a black-handed engineer, happier under the buses than in the office. Alternatively he may spend a good deal of his time working as a driver himself, on the basis that 'the best manure is the farmer's footprints'; like that he will know what is going on in the world outside.

He will know the staff, too, and he may speak the same dialect of English, for the 'gentry' tend to think that running buses, like any other business, is beneath them. (How much of the economic malaise of the country arises from that kind of snobbishness!) Many a bus proprietor has benefitted by being seen to work alongside his drivers, not only through acquiring their respect, but also through finding out what goes on. When Ezra Laycock found that there was too much pilfering, he appointed an inspector (very unusual in country bus firms), and,

115

The depot, with a Leyland of S. Blackwell & Sons (previously with West Riding) at rest in the yard at Earl's Colne, Essex

calling the road staff together, he said: 'There's four wheels to a bus and before it was three wheels for Ezra and one wheel for ye buggers, but now it's one wheel for Ezra and three wheels for ye buggers, so I'm making Walter Snowden Inspector to watch after ye all.'

Even if the boss does much of the maintenance himself, he will probably employ a fitter. The rest of the work will be done by the drivers, as we saw in chapter seven. If the fitter is expected to take more of the responsibility he will probably have a mechanic to help him, and may aspire to the title of engineer himself. These matters of status are extremely subtle, and socially extremely important. Trade representatives soon get a sixth sense that tells them how to handle the situation, but vehicle examiners from the ministry can complicate their own work by failing to appreciate the niceties of it. It is not always easy to distinguish which of the men in boiler suits working on the engine of a Leyland in the yard is the boss, especially if he doesn't speak the way you would expect him to.

What then takes people into this peculiar trade, and what are its satisfactions? The answer to these questions has not, I think, changed greatly over the years since rural public transport first became established, and I doubt whether there would be much difference between the answer of today's busmen and that of the horsemen of past years. Neither would there be that much difference in the nature of the work, save for the shift of technology from the horse to the motor.

116

High standards. A characteristic example of the Mansfield family's Burwell & District fleet, familiar for many years at Cambridge

There would, however, be a much bigger difference in the work, and the satisfactions of the work, if we were to ask these questions of the country busmen on the one hand, and the management and staff of the big town-based companies on the other. For the first great virtue of the situation is the nearness of the country bus business to the community that it serves. Railway closures have produced many scenes of regret and commemoration — I was on the last train on the line from Elsenham when we were played into the terminus by the Thaxted Brass Band, with detonators exploding and every bit of the train crowded with people. (In its last years, the average load could have been carried by a couple of taxis, but it was a most delightful light railway.) But the sadness occasioned by a railway closure is as nothing to the regret that arises when a small country bus firm sells out to the local territorial operator.

Such sales do not usually take place because the traffic has all but faded away, as was the case with so many rural railways. Perhaps the proprietor wants to retire, and has no one to leave the business to. Perhaps it is a matter of death duties. Perhaps it is just an offer that could not be refused, as was the case with Gourd's business, as we saw in chapter four. Whatever the reason, local people have in most cases seen the sale of the local bus company as a loss to their society, and however professional the managers of the big companies may be, this is a very difficult impression to overcome. What is more, it is often justified, because the larger firm will not only have higher costs, but will probably have a formal costing system that disguises the true contribution made by traffic on

117

They didn' 'ave no plaice, Mrs. M., but there's a lovely piece o' 'ake there......

118

country bus services when these are interworked with other kinds of operation. As a result, the services may well be subjected to 'pruning', or long-established timings may be altered to fit into the schedules of a big urban depot.

Not all managers and schedules clerks in the big companies realise how important it is for the market bus to get back to the villages in time to let the housewife get her man's tea when he comes in from work. The finer points of country bus operation, which we looked at in chapter seven, get short shrift when the driver is a stranger from the town, who only comes on the route when the rota causes him to — perhaps once in six weeks. And even the elderly coach that the old operator provided may have been a more satisfactory ride than the low-back, hard seats of the standard Leyland National that has replaced it — a bus, not a coach, and one that seems to have been designed more for ease and economy of maintenance than for comfort.

There may be something more behind this sense of loss that is associated with the transfer of bus services from a small to a large firm. The country bus business can be very much a part of the community it serves. We saw in chapter eight how the reassuring presence of a local driver encouraged people to use coach services even where the train was quicker, but it may not only be the road staff that give the business its local significance. Instead of a remote manager, there

The country bus at home. The Bedford OB with the Duple 'Vista' body, and 29 seats, that was the work-horse of the independents during the post-war years. This one belonged to Miles of Guiting Power, in Gloucestershire

Clockwise from the top

A classic example of road/rail co-ordination. Services like this were not uncommon in the 1920s, but were never encouraged after the railway companies bought their way into the bus industry in 1929

Work out for yourself what the buses do each day, and then ask – what happens on Friday? The attempt to develop sightseeing traffic is interesting

A country firm that set out to provide inter-urban services where there were no railways. The timetable isn't very easy to follow!

This operator is offering an extensive range of extra services – the service had to compete with the buses of the much larger Eastern Counties company

Only an operator with just one service could keep track of all the complications to be found in this timetable, all designed to fit neatly into the pattern of the community that it served

ENTERPRISE BUS SERVICE.   1st OCT. 1946.

STOLFORD - STOGURSEY - BRIDGWATER

	A.M.	A.M.	A.M.	P.M.	P.M.	P.M.	P.M.	P.M.	P.M.
Stolford	8 20	Mon	9 30		1 40	1 40		5 0	5 25
Shurton	8 25	and	9 37		1 47	1 47		5 5	5 30
Burton	8 27	Fri	9 40		1 50	1 50		5 7	5 32
Stogursey	8 30	9 30	9 45		1 55	1 55		5 10	5 40
Stockland	8 40	9 38x	10 0		2 10	2 10		5 20	5 48
Otterhampton	8 45	9 40x	10 5		2 15	2 15	3 10	5 25	5 50
Combwich X Rd.	8 50	9 43			2 20		3 15	5 30	5 55
Combwich Village		9 43	10 10			2 20			
Bridgwater	9 10	10 5	10 30		2 40	2 40	3 35	5 45	6 15
	Mon		Wed.		Mon.	Wed.	Thurs.	Wed.	Tues.
	to		and		and	Fri.	only		Fri.
	Fri.		Sat.		Tues.	Sat.	during		Sat.
	N.W.						School		
							term		

	P.M.	P.M.							
Bridgwater	11 30	12 30	3 0		4 30		4 30	4 30	7 0	9 30
Combwich X Rd.	11 45		3 15		4 50		4 50		7 20	9 50
Combwich Village		12 50	3 18§		4 50			4 46		
Otterhampton	12 20	12 55	3 20x				5 25	4 55	7 25	9 55
Stockland	12 15	1 0	3 22x				5 20	5 0	0	0
Stogursey	11 55	1 15	3 30				5 10	5 10		
Burton	12 0	1 20	3 33*				5 7	5 13		
Shurton	12 3	1 23	3 35*				5 5	5 15		
Stolford	12 10	1 30			5 0		5 0	5 20		
	Mon.	Wed.	Mon.				Mon.	Tues.	Wed.	Tues.
	Tues.	and	Wed.		Wed.		Thurs.	Fri.	Sat.	Fri.
	Thurs.	Sat.	Fri.				N.T.	Sat.		Sat.
	Fri.									T.F.

T.F.   Tuesdays and Fridays leave from Odeon Car Park.
O   Does Not run beyond Otterhampton except to set down Bridgwater Passengers.
N.T.   Not Thursdays During County School Holidays.
N.W.   Not Wednesdays During County School Holidays.   x Stockland Hill.   x Biffen's Corner.
§   Mondays Only.
*   Bridgwater Passengers Only.
   All Buses arriving in Bridgwater to Proceed to Station if Required.
   All Parcels Prepaid MUST BE collected from the Bus.
While every effort will be made to run the service punctually, no responsibility can be accepted for lateness of bus through any cause.
   Proprietor— **K. B. HAYBITTEL,** "Mazoe," Otterhampton.
ESTIMATES GIVEN FOR PRIVATE PARTIES.
'Phone : Combwich 276.

120

To and from Tenbury Wells Every Tuesday.

		a.m.
Hundred House Hotel, leave	..	9 40
Abberley	.. ..	9 45
Stockton	.. ..	9 55
Lowe Green	.. ..	10 0
Eardiston Post Office	..	10 5
Lindridge (Nag's Head)	, ..	10 10
Eastham Bridge	.. ..	10 15
Newnham Bridge..	..	10 20

Via Clows Top		a.m.
Abberley School leave	..	9 40
Pensax	.. ..	9 45
Clows Top ..	..	10 0
Mamble	.. ..	10 5
Broom Inn..	..	10 15

Return from Tenbury 3-30 p.m.

Returning from Market Square, at 3 p.m.

To and from Kidderminster Every Saturday.

		p.m.	p.m.
Menith Wood	..	4 50	..
Pensax	.. ..	5 0	..
Abberley School	..	5 10	6 30
Hundred House Hotel	..	5 15	6 55
Dunley	.. ..	5 35	6 50

Via Bewdley		p.m.
Mamble, leave	.. ..	5 0
Bayton	.. ..	5 10
Clows Top ..	..	5 20
Colliers' Arms	..	5 25
Return from Cape of Good Hope Hotel at 10-30.		

Returning from Green Man Hotel, 9 p.m. Half Moon Hotel, 10.30 p.m.

To and from Worcester Mondays & Saturdays, via Ockeridge.

		a.m.
Martley Rd (Wall House) leave		10 5
,, ,, (Fetlock Lodge)		10 10
Ockeridge	.. .. ,,	10 20

		a.m.
Wichenford	leave ..	10 30
Monkwood Green	,, ..	10 35
Sinton Green	,, ..	10 40
Mosley Turn	,, ..	10 45

Every Wednesday via Martley Hill Side.

		a.m.
Martley Rd (Wall House) leave		10 5
,, ,, (Fetlock Lodge)		10 10
Martley Hill Side	,,	10 15

		a.m.
Wichenford (Malvern View) leave		10 30
Monkwood Green	.. ..	10 35
Sinton Green	.. ..	10 40
Mosley Turn	.. ,,	10 45

Returning from Fruit Market at 3-0 p.m.

The Proprietors will not hold themselves responsible for any loss, inconvenience, or injury in connection with the above Services, but will endeavour to keep times scheduled above, and reserve the right to alter or withdraw any of the above Services without notice.

…S & SATURDAYS to WORCESTER.

..	depart	9 30 a.m.		..	
..		9 35			S
..		9 45		1 0 pm	4 20
el)		9 55		1 5	4 25
..		10 5		1 15	4 35
..		10 15		1 25	4 45
..		10 20		1 30	4 50
..		10 25		1 35	4 55
St. about		10 45		1 50	5 15

…dred House at 4.25 Saturdays only.

…S & SATURDAYS from WORCESTER.

..	depart	11 30 a.m.	3 0 p.m.	5 30 p.m.
..		11 50	3 20	5 50
..		11 55	3 25	5 55
..		12 0	3 30	6 0
..		12 10	3 40	6 10
el)		12 20	3 50	6 20
..		12 30	4 5	6 30

…h Pensax, Clows Top and Cleobury Mortimer.
…rdays runs through to Pensax and Clows Top.

…and Worcester Every Monday.

…otel) depart	..	..	9 0 a.m.
…gel Street, arrive		..	9 30
			10 45
), Angel Street, depart		..	5 30 p.m.

…derminster Every Thursday.

a.m.		Via Bewdley.		a.m.
9 15		Feather Bed Lane	.. ..	8 55
9 5		Broom Inn..	..	9 0
9 20		Mamble (Sun Inn)	..	9 10
9 35		Clows Top ..	..	9 25
9 40		Colliers' Arms	..	9 30
.0 5				

…el, Returning from Half Moon Hotel at 4-0 p.m.

…' MOTOR COACH SERVICES

…AM—HISTON—CAMBRIDGE

A.M.	A.M.	A.M.	A.M.	P.M.	P.M.	P.M.	P.M.	P.M.	P.M.	P.M.	P.M.
8 25	9 30	10 25	11 30	1 30	2 15	3 5	4 0	5 15	5 40	6 0	7 0
8 45	9 50	10 45	11 50	1 50	2 35	3 25	4 20	5 35	6 0	6 20	7 20
9 10	9 15	11.0	12 15	2 15	3 0	3 50	4 45	6 0		6 45	7 45
											C

A.M.	A M	NOON	P.M	P.M	P.M	P.M.	P.M	P M	P M	P M	P M
10.15	11.10	12.0	1.15	2.15	3.15	3.35	4.15	5.15	..	6.10	6 55
10.40	11.35	12.25	12.40	2.40	3.40	4.0	4.40	5.40	6.0	6.35	7.20
11.0	11.55	12.45	1.0	3.0	4.0	4.20	5.0	6.0	6.20	6.55	7.40
			A			B			C		

	P.M
)	11 0
S	11.25
S	11.45

School Term only   C Not on Saturdays   D Not on Mondays

…own in Histon   Special Parties catered for and Estimates given for
…s or Letters undertaken in or out of Histon or Cambridge. Tickets
…ked if Patrons place their order by Tuesday of each week.

…ble prices and the convenience of Patrons is my object, and
…r your confidence and encouragement.

Dunmow, Rodings, Ongar and Brentwood. Daily Service.

days only.		a.m.	p.m.	p.m.	p.m.	Satur. a.m.
Dunmow	.. dep	9 15	5 0	9 0	..
High Roding	,,	9 25	5 10	9 10	..
Leaden Roding	,,	9 35	5 20	9 20	..
White Roding	,,	9 45	5 30	..	..
Abbess Roding	,,	9 50	5 35	..	..
Fyfield	,,	10 0	5 45	..	..
Ongar	,,	10 10	5 55	..	..
Kelvedon Common	,,	10 20	6 5	..	..
Pilgrims Hatch	,,	10 25	6 10	..	..
Brentwood	arr	10 30	6 15	..	..

Brentwood	.. dep	1 30	7 30	..
Pilgrims Hatch	,,	1 35	7 35	..
Kelvedon Common	,,	1 40	7 40	..
Ongar	,,	1 50	7 50	..
Fyfield	,,	2 0	8 0	..
Abbess Roding	,,	2 10	8 10	..
White Roding	,,	2 15	8 15	..
Leaden Roding	,,	8 30	2 25	8 25	8 30
High Roding	,,	8 40	2 35	8 35	8 40
Dunmow	arr	8 50	2 45	8 45	8 50

Sundays only.		a.m.	p.m.	p.m.	p.m.	a.m.	p.m.	p.m.	p.m.
		9 15	1 0	7 30	10 45	9 15	1 0	7 30	10 30
		9 25	1 10	7 40	10 55	9 25	1 10	7 40	10 40
		9 35	1 20	7 50	11 5	9 35	1 20	7 50	10 50
		9 45	1 30	8 0	..	9 45	1 30	8 0	..
		9 50	1 35	8 5	..	9 50	1 35	8 5	..
		10 0	1 45	8 15	..	10 0	1 45	8 15	..
		10 10	1 55	8 25	..	10 10	1 55	8 25	..
		10 20	2 5	8 35	..	10 20	2 5	8 35	..
		10 25	2 10	8 40	..	10 25	2 10	8 40	..
		10 30	2 15	8 45	..	10 30	2 15	8 45	..

		10 45	4 0	9 0		10 50	2 20	9 15
		10 50	5 5	9 35		10 55	2 25	9 20
		10 55	5 10	9 40		11 0	2 30	9 25
		11 5	5 20	9 50		11 10	2 40	9 35
		11 15	5 30	10 0		11 20	2 50	9 45
		11 25	5 40	10 10		11 30	3 0	9 55
		11 30	5 45	10 15		11 35	3 5	10 0
		11 40	5 55	10 25	8 45	11 45	3 15	10 10
		11 50	6 5	10 35	8 55	11 55	3 25	10 20
		12 0	6 15	10 45	9 5	12 5	3 35	10 30

This service runs in connection with our Stortford and Chelmsford Services.
Also a five minutes service from Brentwood to London.
On all Bank Holiday Mondays a Sunday Service will run.

FOR FARES SEE BACK PAGE.

Messrs. C. Simpson & Sons will endeavour to maintain the services enumerated in this Time Table, but they give no guarantee that same shall be performed, and they reserve the right to alter, suspend, or withdraw the running of any vehicle or service without notice.

Messrs. C. Simpson & Sons will not be liable for any loss, damage, injury or inconvenience that any passenger may sustain, for any failure to carry out the same, or for want of punctuality in the service.

All enquiries and suggestions for the improvement of the service should be addressed to Messrs. C. Simpson & Sons, Leaden Roding.

Chelmsford and Bishops Stortford.

		M	S	T O	T O	F O	M T	F O	M F
		a m	a m	p m	p m	p m	p m	p m	p m
Chelmsford	dep	..	..	12 30	2 30	4 30	5 0	7 40	9 30
Hare & Hounds	,,	..	..	12 40	2 40	4 40	5 10	7 50	9 40
Cross Keys	,,	..	..	12 45	2 45	4 45	5 15	7 55	9 45
Fountain	,,	..	..	12 55	2 55	4 55	5 25	8 5	9 55
Leaden Roding	,,	6 0	..	1 0	3 0	5 0	5 30	8 10	10 0
High Roding		..	..	..	..	..	..	4 25	..
White Roding	,,	10 11	45	..	..	2 40	..	..
Hatfield 3rd Oak.	,,	20 11	55	..	..	2 50	4 10	..
Hatfield Heath	,,	30 12	5	1 50	..	3 0	4 20	..
Hallingbury	,,	35 12	10	1 55	..	3 4	25	..
Bishops Stortford	arr	45 12	20	2 5	..	3 15	4 30	..

Bishops Stortford and Chelmsford.

	T	MS	T O	T O	F O	F O	MS
	a m	a m	p m	p m	p m	p m	p m
Bishops Stortford	dep	..	9 0	11	0	1 30	..	3 30	5 0
Hallingbury	,,	..	9 10	11	10	1 40	..	3 40	5 10
Hatfield Heath	,,	..	9 15	11	15	1 45	..	3 45	5 15
Hatfield 3rd Oak,	,,	..	9 26	..	..	..	..	..	5 25
White Roding	,,	..	9 35	11	25	..	..	3 55	5 35
High Roding	,,	..	9 30	..	..	..	..	..	..
Leaden Roding	,,	9 45	9 45	..	..	10 10	1 15	4	5 45
Fountain	,,	..	..	..	..	10 15	1 25	4	5 50
Cross Keys	,,	..	10 0	..	..	10 20	1 40	4	5 55
Hare & Hounds	,,	..	10 5	..	..	10 25	1 45	4	6 0
Chelmsford	arr	..	10 15	..	..	10 45	2 0	4	6 15

MS—Monday to Saturday.   TO—Thursday only.
MF—Friday.   FO—Friday.
MT—Thursday.   T—Tuesday.

Messrs. C. Simpson & Sons will endeavour to maintain the services enumerated in this Time Table, but they give no guarantee that same shall be performed, and they reserve the right to alter, suspend, or withdraw the running of any vehicle or service without notice.

Messrs. C. Simpson & Sons will not be liable for any loss, damage, injury or inconvenience that any passenger may sustain, for any failure to carry out the same, or for want of punctuality in the service.

All enquiries and suggestions for the improvement of the service should be addressed to Messrs. C. Simpson & Sons, Leaden Roding.

Bishops Stortford.

Saturday Only.			Sunday only.		
pm	pm	pm	pm	pm	pm	pm	pm
1 40	5 15	6 30	7 30	8 45	9 10	1 40	5 15	6 30	9 10
1 50	5 30	6 45	7 45	9 0	9 25	1 50	5 30	6 45	9 25
1 55	5 35	6 50	7 50	9 5	9 30	1 55	5 35	6 50	9 30
2 5	5 40	6 55	7 55	9 15	9 40	2 5	5 40	6 55	9 40
2 10	5 45	7 0	8 0	9 15	11 0	2 10	5 45	7 0	9 45
6 0	7 10		11 10		6 0	7 10	
2 30	7 20		11 30		2 30	7 20	
2 40	7 30		11 50		2 40	7 30	
2 45	7 35		12 5		2 45	7 35	

On all Bank Holiday Mondays a Sunday Service will run.

FOR FARES SEE BACK PAGE.

AGENT:
H. MILLER,
TOBACCONIST AND CONFECTIONER,
28, South Street, BISHOPS STORTFORD, Herts.

We've climbed the hill, but what's it done to the radiator? One of the late Charles Klapper's inimitable vignettes of Shropshire bus operation. The war-time 'utility' Bedford was in Carpenter's fleet

will usually be a local man who is in charge — someone who is known in the pub, or who in earlier days might have been known in the chapel. It may be easy to deride the 'human touch', but it is what makes up that figure on the balance sheet that accountants call 'goodwill', which the large firms pay good money for, and then so often throw away.

The other side of the coin is the nature of the job. The manager in the local office of the big company may be able to work a nine-to-five day; his superior may enjoy a five-day week. In the small firm the boss is never 'off duty'. If he is not driving, or struggling with a recalcitrant alternator, or doing tomorrow's orders, he is still working — even when he is in a village pub, or chatting with the drivers in the yard. Every little detail matters. Which of the men to send on a coach hire for the local Women's Institute is a decision based upon his knowledge of their personalities, including their relative ability to attract tips. You don't *ask* a man what tips he is getting, but somehow you know. In the same way you know what the opposition is charging for private parties to popular destinations, so that you can assess how far you can ease your own prices up without risking losing your regular customers. In the textbooks it is called market intelligence, but for the small proprietor it is the skill of survival.

And so it has always been. The 1920s busman, backing his judgement with his war service gratuity and buying a Ford or a Chevrolet, and starting a service

Carpenter's Leyland Tiger – both vehicle and staff unmistakably pre 'New Look'

through half a dozen villages, built up his business with just these skills. A remarkable number of them seem to have survived, only to sell out in the 1930s, 1950s or 1960s. What kept them going, despite the long hours and the responsibility, was partly a desire for independence, partly the attraction of making a living doing something you enjoy. Many of them seem to have sold up with regret, and some have found it difficult to enjoy their retirement. For there is a non-monetary satisfaction to be had in the trade, which keeps people in it who might well earn more elsewhere — and it applies to many drivers as well as to those who employ them.

Not that money should be neglected. If your wealth is tied up in your business, you will take a close interest in the cash that comes in. There is no big money to be made in running buses, and for many small businessmen in country bus firms, the annual visit to the accountant to examine the balance sheet is not to be looked forward to as an unmixed pleasure. But there is a basic satisfaction about seeing the cash come in, especially where there are local services where people pay with real money — the education authority's cheque may be more important, but the cash bag emptied on the counter has a symbolic quality about it. So there is about the trip to the bank with the takings — a weekly ritual that men have felt the miss of, after retirement.

But when all is said, there is something about running buses that is enjoyable

An anonymous Dodge decays quietly at the back of someone's yard

for its own sake, and there is the added satisfaction of knowing the little world within which the buses and coaches you run play an important part. It may not be a conscious satisfaction, but that makes it no less real. It is certainly more easily felt in the rural community than it is in the anonymity of the town. And it may be something more.

It may be something that readers of this book are already aware of. Associated with the past it is nostalgia, but within it there is a sharp awareness of the sights and sounds — and smells — of the bus business. The whine of a Bedford engine in low gear; the sheer sense of power that emanates from a diesel engine, even when it is idling in a stationary vehicle; the labouring sound of an engine on a long upward gradient, and the feeling of relief as the driver shifts into top gear when he is over the crest — all these and many more impressions are part of the busman's trade. There has always been something special about having your name in neat lettering low down on the nearside panel, or neatly scrolled on the rear of the coach.

Speedsure
Prop^s J.Hibbs & Bray
Underall wt.

10   A Suffolk Story

When I was a young man I had the unforgettable experience of managing a country bus business, jointly with my partner, the late Bert Davidson, for four years that were to prove some of the happiest, and most frustrating, of my life. Happiest because of the nature of the work and the community of which I found myself a part; most frustrating because at the end, my partner having died, I was unable to carry the firm through an unforeseen economic blizzard that came just when our financial circumstances were at their most vulnerable.

The full story of running Corona Coaches I hope to tell in another book, but here I may perhaps be permitted to share memories with others, and through them recreate once more the sense of what it is like to be managing, working on and riding in the country bus. I hope this will be something a bit more than self-indulgent nostalgia, for there are insights to be gained from this experience as well as bitter-sweet memories of country sights, sounds and smells, and those of the buses too.

Corona Coaches was not untypical in its origins — a certain Nathan Chinery had set up as a carrier in the Suffolk village of Acton in the nineteenth century, and when his son Alan returned from World War I he 'mechanised' the business, developing both goods and passenger work. Acton, as the map will show, lies just outside the market town of Sudbury, above the valley of the River Stour, which here forms the boundary between Essex and Suffolk. Alan and his wife called their first coach the *Joybelle,* but it seems to have been preceded by at least one charabanc. When several of the drivers had been prosecuted for exceeding the speed limit — 12mph in those days — Alan decided to take a party to Felixstowe himself. The Ipswich to Felixtowe road was notorious for speed traps, but what irked Alan most when he was convicted was that the evidence came from a constable who had paced him at 14mph, on a bicycle.

In due course a regular local service was established between Acton and Sudbury, on Thursdays (the local market-day) and Saturdays. There was no half holiday for farm labourers then, and two round trips were made on Saturday evenings, to get to the shops. For some years this service and private hire work accounted for the passenger side of the business, but there was work for the lorries, much of it in connection with the chemical essence factory of Stafford Allen, down in the Stour Valley, and the horsehair factory in the nearby village of Glemsford. The drivers worked on the coaches or the lorries as demand required.

The Chinerys' business might have remained like that, for there were numerous other bus operators in the area. The Stour acted as the boundary between two territorial bus companies, Eastern National and Eastern Counties, and in such a situation it was usual for the private firms to be left alone. But Alan Chinery saw an opportunity for expansion with the development of the new express coach services, and in May 1929 he started a service from Stowmarket to London, calling at a string of villages with no rail service, and then, as we have seen, offering a quality of service that people preferred to the train at places like Lavenham, Long Melford, Sudbury, Halstead and Braintree. The fares from Sudbury and the neighbouring villages were 4s 6d (22½p) single, 6s (30p) day return and 8s 6d (42½p) period return — not all that cheap, when farm labourers got 9d (3p) an hour for overtime, when it was available.

Alan and his wife decided that 'Corona' would be a good title for the firm's crowning achievement, and so Corona Coaches (A. Chinery, Proprietor) was born. For the first year, the finances of the London service were a worry, and there was pressure from some of those who had backed it to give it up. But in its second season it began to flourish, and by the time the licensing laws were introduced in 1931 there were two journeys each way every day (which meant keeping one coach in London), and feeder services had been put on to bring people in to join the main service at Sudbury.

When Bert Davidson and I took over in 1956 things had not changed much. The local service had been added to by a market-day run to Ipswich and a twice weekly picture bus from Lavenham through Acton to Sudbury. After various attempts to build up the Sudbury–Halstead section, there was just a 'dishy bus'

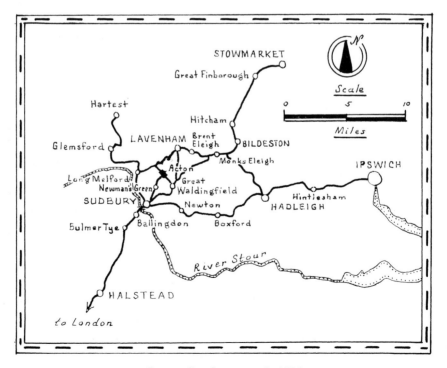

Corona Coaches routes in 1956

Dual-purpose vehicles like this were to be found in the period immediately after World War I – the Corona example stands outside the 'Crown' at Acton, Suffolk

that supplemented the London journeys on Saturdays. An excursion licence permitted day trips to seaside resorts from Sudbury and a few local villages, together with circular tours.

There were eleven coaches in the fleet, and a staff of nine drivers, one conductor and a fitter, with a manager and a clerk in the office. Several of the older men had worked on local farms, and most of them lived in the village — one, of course, lived in London. The premises at Acton consisted of a house, with a wooden office beside it and a workshop (complete with inspection pit) behind; across the road, next to the Crown there was a yard with petrol and diesel storage and a bus running shed, capable of sheltering eight coaches (and with another pit). This was adequate, because three of the vehicles were out-stationed: one in London, one in Stowmarket and one at Hadleigh. The conductor went as far as Chelmsford with the up coach in the morning, and came back with the 9am from King's Cross; then he did a second round trip to Braintree and back in the afternoon. On his rest-day, one of the drivers took his place. The two London drivers had a bit of extra status, in that they never worked in the yard, but the others would take their turn to put on overalls and wash down the coaches, or help the mechanic if they had some mechanical ability. One of them was responsible for the steam-cleaning machine, and another was our tyre fitter.

Some 12 years later, and professional coaching standards have been achieved with this neat Morris Commercial, new to the firm in 1932

A few months after we acquired the business — by this time already a limited company — we were approached by Harry Rippingale, whose stage and excursion licences and four vehicles we acquired in May 1956. By careful re-scheduling I was able to cover the whole combined mileage with only ten coaches, which was how the deal had been financed. In a later merger we acquired the bus operations of Eddie Long of Glemsford, thus taking us into Bury St Edmunds. But let us start with the business as it existed in February 1956.

The Corona fleet could be divided simply into petrol and diesel coaches. Naturally it was the diesels that were mainly used on the London service, since they were best suited to the substantial annual mileage that it required. Three of the four were already looking out of date in 1956 — they were the two sister machines, the Leyland PS1/1 Tigers and the AEC Regal III. These all had half-cab forward control layout, which by that time had been made obsolete by the underfloor engines that permitted a higher seating capacity. The two Leylands had 35-seat bodies by Gurney Nutting, while the Regal had a 33-seat body by Windover — it is remarkable how many body-builders there were in this country in the post-war years. In the ordinary way Charlie Gilson had one or other of the Tigers at the London end, while Harry Pleasants (known to us all as Jokey) had the Regal, which was kept in Stowmarket. When it was necessary to bring either of them in for servicing, or for the ministry vehicle-examiners to inspect them, we had to ask the passengers to change at the garage at Acton — this was best done on a Wednesday, which was always the quietest day. Re-fuelling, on the other hand, could be done at Acton with the passengers still in their seats, which would not have been possible with petrol vehicles.

By 1956 those coaches had done six or seven years' service, and they were still good for many more. The round trip on the London service came to 150 miles, which meant a total of more than 2,000 miles a week, or 104,000 miles a year, to be shared between the three coaches. (For their drivers it was less, because of rest-days and holidays, but for both men and machines it was a considerable task.) No petrol-engined vehicle could have stood the strain of such high mileage, and the diesels were treated with respect almost amounting to affection by the men. I think it speaks volumes for the quality of the British coaches of that period that they could be operated with total reliability without any of the sophistication of the professional engineer — but it says just as much for the skill and responsibility of the company's qualified fitter, 'Bunkie' Chisnall.

The fourth diesel was really an oddity. Alan Chinery had always been a progressive operator — in the pre-war years he had owned an AEC 'Q' (such as we came across in chapter five). The Corona 'Q' was only a 32-seater, which hardly gave the benefit in capacity that the engine layout was intended to provide, but Alan seems to have hankered after the unusual, and his first underfloor coach came in 1952: an AEC Regal IV with a 41-seat body, again by Gurney Nutting. ECF 305 was a most peculiar choice for service work, though, for the door was placed halfway along the nearside, so that when working on London or an excursion, the driver had to get up and go half way down the coach to let passengers get on or off. (Added to this, ECF had quite the heaviest sliding door it has ever been my experience to manhandle — quite beyond the capacity of an elderly passenger to open or close.) A body layout like this would be ideal for touring, but on most Thursdays the 41-seater was needed, with a relief, for the Sudbury market service, where (as we saw in chapter seven) there would be twelve stops in the length of Acton village street.

ECF was different also in having a semi-automatic transmission. One of the evocative sounds of my experience has always been the long, slow double-declutch gear-change, which could often tell you what vehicle it was that was coming round the corner. There was a satisfaction, too, in the achievement of a successful, smooth gear-change, with the engine speed neatly matched with the road speed, and everything falling exactly into place. (The consequences of failure are best not recalled.) But ECF had what in pre-war days would have been called a preselector gearbox — you kept a knob on the steering column in the slot for the next gear you would require, and then when you came to change, you pressed a trip lever on the floor with your foot, which operated a pneumatic device that changed the gear for you. (One consequence was the need for an expensive compressor, which was one more thing to go wrong — although it is fair to say it seldom did so.) The younger drivers liked the system, but we discovered that some of the older men had not been instructed in its use, and tended to try and double-declutch with the trip lever.

If ECF was a bit of a monster — all else apart, it was remarkably heavy, with substantial and very comfortable seats — the rest of the fleet was more characteristic of the period. All the other vehicles were Bedfords, and all were petrol-driven; four of them were the true work-horses of the country bus firm of the period, 29-seater normal control coaches which went by the name chosen by the firm that built bodies for most of them — the Vista. Invented by the Duple company, it became a generic title, in the way that Thermos did for the vacuum flask, and Biro for the ball-point pen. It was really a basically sound design for a coach body to fit the Bedford OB chassis, which could equally well be bodied as a van; it was good-looking, and of a very convenient size. Various other body-builders copied the Duple model, and the trade tended to call their products all by the same title — the Vista.

We had four, and only two of them were bodied by Duple. One of the others, on a Bedford HML chassis, was built by a firm called Lucas, about which little is known, but the second — delivered at the same time as the Regal III — was bodied by that traditional supplier to country operators, Thurgood of Ware. CCF 462 had one of the stoutest body frames I ever saw. I had to go out to an accident one day, when a lorry jack-knifed on the hill at Boxford, and collided with the offside front pillar. It was only then that I realised the quality as well as the dimensions of the timber that Thurgood had used, for the pillar, although fractured, had not broken. The driver might not have owed his life to that, but it certainly saved him from injury. I was the more impressed because it was well known that certain body-builders were not above using green timber in those difficult post-war years. Thurgood had been a country bus operator himself, running the People's Motor Services, which was to become part of the London Transport green bus undertaking; he was also involved in commercial aviation. I came that day to hold a very high opinion of the product of his works at Ware.

The Bedford Vista had the advantage of being an all-purpose vehicle. With coach-type seats it could hold its own with most 'luxury coaches' of the period, yet with lighter frames its seats could be suitable for stage carriage work. Either way, we used the Vistas for all types of operation: reliefs on the London service; local bus services on quiet days; excursions of all kinds, and private hire. The engine was simple and sturdy, and later on, when we were running seven of these coaches, I found an airfield in the heart of Suffolk where ex-military stock was on offer, so I bought several engines at the knock-down price of £7 10s (£7.50). With them at the back of the workshop it was easy to deal with mechanical problems by changing engines, and getting the coach back on the road — very important in busy summer traffic, when at least once we worked into the small hours to do it.

Though we did not know it, the days of the 29-seater were numbered. In my view the bus and coach industry has followed a mistaken policy for the past thirty-five years, seeking ever larger vehicles for all purposes. All the expected advantages in labour productivity can so easily be lost through lack of flexibility, and especially through the loss of frequency (though that is more of an urban problem). In the mid 1950s there was room for something a bit bigger, though, and already the underfloor engine had produced a standard design for diesel vehicles that gave forty-one seats in coach formation, or forty-three at least with closer-packed bus-type frames and upholstery. But the new coaches were expensive, and there were still problems with the under-slung engine, such as the tendency for fuel or water pipes to fracture. (The forward-mounted engine in the half-cab coach or double-decker was also a good deal more accessible for maintenance and running repairs.) In a period of change, various attempts will be made to satisfy the market, and Bedford developed a new series of chassis for which Duple designed bodywork with the title of Vega.

We had three of these to begin with, with 33, 37 and 38 seats respectively, each one heavier and more of a luxury coach than its predecessor. They too could take their turn on the London service — DGV 123, the 33-seater, served on the Hadleigh outstation for some years, and was first reserve to carry on up the London road as a relief on days when the service car was overloaded. (The London service acted as a local bus at the country end, so that loadings could not always be controlled by pre-booking, and anyhow we never turned passengers away.) DGV was a bit austere, though, and the 37- and 38-seaters were the vehicles that did most of the up-market private hire work, and the new types of excursion that we found a market for, to places like Woburn Abbey or London Airport and Windsor. (We sold DGV, along with the ex-Rippingale vehicles, to finance the takeover of Rippingale's business.)

The trouble with the Vegas was that we could never get dispensation to use them on stage services without a conductor. Although they were normal control, the front-mounted engine meant that the door had to be set back, whereas in the Vista the driver sat almost in line with it. In our traffic area the

The Hadleigh and Hartest coaches await arrival of the London service at Old Market Place, Sudbury, early in 1956

commissioners were prepared to endorse the road service licence for a country route to allow 'front-entrance normal control vehicles with a maximum of twenty-nine seats' to be used without a conductor, which would otherwise have been permissible only where there were twenty seats or less, as we saw in chapter five.

This was an enormous advantage when we began to expand our stage service activities, partly by the acquisition of the Rippingale business, but also as a result of recasting the London timetable. This gave passengers a better day-return facility, and improved weekend workings so as to get a broader spread of traffic, but it meant that some of the local traffic that had used the London coaches would have been deprived of a service, so we found ourselves running a number of journeys that were pretty thin. Like all country firms, we set out to cater for them by working them into a generally profitable duty, because when you have brought a driver on, you have got to pay his wages for the guaranteed day, and like that the true costs of some of the journeys could be covered by a much smaller load of passengers than you might expect. Even so, the afternoon run to Bildeston and back could be a lonely task if it wasn't market-day, and certainly did not warrant a big bus with a conductor. It was a typical 'd/c' (driver conduct) duty (which today would be 'one-man operated', or even — save the mark — 'one-person operated'), and Billy Bird, the shop steward, christened it the 'doddle'.

The usual problem with the bigger Bedfords was the gearbox. Starting away on the level with a 29-seater, even with a load of passengers, it was possible — though not desirable — to use the second gear. The same practice with a 37-seater was not to be recommended, but the drivers found it difficult to remember. The result was still a smooth start, for that is the mark of a skilled driver, and no one would allow himself to fail that test, but it did burn out the clutch. I think it may have had something to do with the typical whine of the Bedford engine in the lower gears, that is a never to be forgotten memory of the breed. It could tend to set your teeth on edge, and encourage you to get through the gears as quickly as you could.

Later, when Eddie Long joined our board and we took over his fleet and services, we found ourselves with double-deckers. Long's navy blue and white vehicles were repainted in our tangerine and chocolate as quickly as possible, but we altered the fleet name on the side to read 'Corona' instead of 'Corona Coaches' for the three deckers — a Bristol, an AEC Regent and a Guy Arab II. We did the same for our only single-decker bus — CLA 103, known inevitably as *Clara*. This was a Leyland LT7, with a box-like body by Eastern Coach Works that I think had not been on the chassis originally — Eddie had bought it from Birch Brothers, but its earlier history is unknown to me. With *Clara* and the deckers we lost a lot of the flexibility that had been an advantage, but now we had a busy stage service from Clare into Sudbury, extended in the peaks to

A Corona coach in a spot of bother at Hadleigh, Suffolk, in the 1930s

serve the factory at Sible Hedingham, from which the buses took a lonely route over a disused airfield to come back through Clare and Glemsford to Sudbury again.

But the pride of the fleet was KGV 195, an AEC Reliance with a Burlingham 41-seater body, which we had ordered to our own specification for the London service. It was a true dual-purpose vehicle, having a bus-type body, with mechanically driven jack-knife doors, but it was fitted with full luxury seats and had a large boot. Bert had the sensible idea of having 7ft 6in (2.3m) standard seats fitted into the 8ft (2.4m) wide body, and offset from the side panels, which gave a noticeable extra space for passengers' comfort. We also specified an exhaust brake, worked by a small flap mounted on the normal brake pedal, so that it came into action before the wheel-brakes, and often avoided the need to use them; we soon showed a significant saving on brake and clutch pads. KGV became the usual vehicle for the up London service, driven by Jokey, but was much liked by the other men, including Bill Swindells, the leading driver, and Bill Sandford, the 'honorary tyre fitter'.

Unlike most small country bus firms, we came to have sufficient stage carriage work to justify set duties, which made the process of making out the daily orders a lot simpler. On Saturdays there were two duties that I designed specially to conduct myself, arranged so that I could be in and out of the office at Sudbury during the day, to keep an eye on the bookings for Sunday, and — late in the afternoon — to type out Sunday's orders, which went up to the garage at Acton on the five o'clock coach. On busy weekends this meant watching the London charts, or deciding whether to cancel an excursion that seemed to be loading badly, or whether to run a second coach if another one was loading well. At bank holiday times, and on some other busy weekends, it meant deciding whether to hire coaches from other firms, to provide reliefs on the London service.

Inter-hiring we have seen to be a common practice among country bus firms, and there were several neighbouring operators upon whom we could call. The Easter weekend was the busiest of the year; it was as if people who had stayed at home all the winter made this their first break of the year, and either came down from London to stay with their relatives in the country, or the other way about. Duplicates were wanted from the Thursday evening, and everyone wanted to go home on the Monday, when we ran a Sunday service. The logistics of that movement were complex, and it was not until the 9am from London came in on Monday that we could be quite sure how many day-return passengers there would be to add to the weekenders on the up journeys that evening.

Through the inter-hiring process we got to know other operators' coaches as well as our own. Some of them were first call for us — Beestons of Hadleigh worked for us whenever we needed them, and could be relied on to provide the service coach from the Hadleigh spur, often with 'young Ben' himself at the wheel. Their fleet of light brown coaches was always beautifully turned out, and it was almost like having one of our own vehicles on the service when we hired one of Beestons. Newton Rule of Boxford could be relied on to help out, usually with a Vega, and Taylor's half-cab 35-seater was often hired to work a relief from Bildeston. In the days before Eddie Long merged his business with ours, he could work the Hartest spur if we were pressed, or a relief from Lavenham.

For all of these firms, the villages were the heartland from which the traffic came. Even Sudbury, with a population of 8,000 or so, was a part of the country, and none of the local firms had a garage there. Only the combine company, Eastern Counties, kept a couple of buses in an outstation. H. C. Chambers & Son came through on their service between Colchester and Bury St. Edmunds, with neat red buses, including some double-deckers, but their garage was about eight miles south, in the middle of the village at Bures. Much of the local traffic between Sudbury and Long Melford was carried by Theobald's service, worked in those days largely with small green coaches — on market-days and Saturday afternoons they seemed to leave as soon as they were loaded. They were kept in a typical village street garage, in Melford's long High Street.

Then there were the true country bus firms, often rather secretive. Amos came in from the Belchamps — I never saw a copy of his timetable. Honeywood had a workman's service from Stanstead, on which he used a petrol-engined Leyland double-decker — word had it that Leylands eventually bought it back from him for their museum, as it was the last one still running. Norfolk of Nayland had some odd journeys into the town, and some vintage, beautifully kept coaches, in a rich green livery; they were the oldest established of the local firms. A rare bird, which we met in chapter four, would be one of Jennings' Olympics, taking a rest from his London service. But above all I remember Harry Rippingale, in the days before he sold us his business, sitting on the front seat of a 20-seater Bedford as the passengers got off, collecting their fares in a pudding basin. 'Thankye m'dear,' he would say. 'See ye when y'cum back me old dear' — he knew each one of them by name, so why bother with tickets?

Rippingale's largest vehicle had been a 29-seater Bedford, and one of the advantages we had with rather larger coaches was to avoid the need for reliefs. But the small coaches so common in the area had been sensible in the days before we got to know that delectable corner of the world, when the lanes were narrow and winding, with high hedges and little room to manoeuvre. So it was not surprising that some of the villages were very late in getting a bus service. During my years running Corona, and the final year when I was working for Jack Mulley, I was able to provide the first service to three such villages: Preston St Mary in Suffolk, Great Henny and Middleton in Essex.

Even today, when I am in Sudbury, I can walk down Market Hill and recognise faces from those days: faces of former passengers. I can think of few callings more satisfying than to provide country bus services, when it is a small firm you are running, and you, and those who share in the work, are part of the community you serve. I know many of those who work in the big firms, both managers and road staff, and I have a respect for their professionalism, but I suspect that a good many of them would envy my experience. Even now I have been known to sling a bag and punch over my shoulders, and climb into the Regal III; sliding the door shut and giving the bell a double press is all one movement, and as Bill Sandford pulls away from Old Market Place with the 6pm to Lavenham I start round my passengers. But that is only in a dream.

11   Some Problems

The years of prosperity for the country bus were from 1945 to some time about ten years later, when services were being expanded, both by adding new routes and by running on extra days on the old ones. Proprietors who had sold their businesses to the combine for a few hundred pounds in the 1930s must have regretted their lack of foresight — yet who could have been expected to possess it? Others who accepted offers from the British Transport Commission after 1947 did not do so badly.

The reasons for the boom were diverse. One was increased purchasing power, partly because agricultural wages had risen (though not as much as industrial wages) during the war, but this was offset by a trend for farms to shed labour as mechanisation and consolidation proceeded, and the combine harvester began to replace the reaping-machine. Another was the healthy demand for labour in the small towns, both for industry and the service trades and professions. Income from this went far to offset the changes in agricultural employment, for there were small factories wanting hands; shops wanting salespeople; and offices wanting clerks and typists. The typical country bus service, running on market-day and Saturday, now might acquire a commuter journey each way on five days a week, or even six.

But the additional purchasing power had limited outlets. Food rationing continued until 1954, which meant that household spending was limited by the quantities permitted, and while village people had been able to supplement their diet during the war from local produce, this was not the same thing as being able to buy as much meat or cheese as the family wanted. Clothes rationing continued, too, and for part of the post-war period the 'basic' petrol ration was discontinued (due to balance of payments problems), so that even those who owned cars were limited in their use. Bus operators, on the other hand, had petrol sufficient for their service needs, coloured with a dye to prevent it from being sold on the black market.

It was thus that travel became one of the limited ways in which money could be spent, and for some ten years the country buses were full, taking people to look for lower prices and greater choice in one town or another, and to look for recreation and entertainment at the seaside or the cinema. The small, normal control coaches of the private firms, some of them twenty years old, Fords, Bedfords, Morris-Commercials, Austins and even the occasional Reo, all these were kept busy as never before. New coaches and buses were few and far between, though in one or two cases rural operators had been able to obtain 'unfrozen' chassis, which Guy, Bristol and Daimler had been allowed to produce in small quantities after 1942. (These usually had double-deck bodies of an angu-

136

Osborne's Bedford, with a war-time utility body, makes the connection at Witham station, replacing the Essex light railway which had itself succumbed to the competition of the bus

lar 'utility' design, and their seating and interior trim well deserved the contemporary epithet 'austerity', for wooden slatted seats now returned. A few such uncompromising machines took the form of normal control buses, looking like a parody of the Vista style.)

Some forward-looking operators had placed orders when war broke out for new coaches to be delivered as and when available, and they were given a head start. The increase in demand called for larger vehicles, too, and the half-cab coach or bus, seating 33, 35 or occasionally 37 passengers (the latter with austerity seating) began to be used more and more on such routes as would take them — the highway authorities and the farmers had hardly begun the reconstruction of the country roads that made them fit for full-sized buses. Sometimes the traffic was sufficient to justify a double-decker: Premier Travel acquired from Gill's Coaches a twice-weekly service from Godmanchester to Bedford, by way of Huntingdon and St Neots and numerous villages, and in the early 1950s the demand for this was enough for a 53-seater decker. That was a far cry from the small country buses that Mr Gill had run in the 1930s — and even farther from the present, for the service has now entirely disappeared, along with the company's Godmanchester depot.

By the late 1950s the rural transport problem was becoming serious enough for a departmental committee to examine it. I was one of those who gave evidence, perhaps because of my recent direct experience, when the fall in demand undermined the finances of the Corona services. The atmosphere at the hearing was friendly, but I felt the committee was far from possessing the true feel of the country bus business — as is always the case when bus services are debated, those who talk about them seldom experience them at first hand. I was already convinced that the great weakness of the situation was the dog-in-the-manger attitude of the territorial companies, whether state-owned or not, who had no notion of letting local firms, with their markedly lower costs, relieve them of their 'unremunerative' services. I said as much to W. T. James of British Electric Traction, the only busman on the committee, and he had the grace to look uncomfortable, but the outcome was a recommendation for government subsidy. One of those who gave evidence on the same day was David St John Thomas, so that the Jack Committee benefitted me by introducing me to a long-term friend as well as publisher.

The Jack Report was a dead letter, so far as tackling the rural bus problem was concerned. If I had had the experience and training in traffic costing that I later received while working for British Rail, I would have taken further the issue of the grossly inadequate costing then practised by the territorial bus companies; I did raise the issue with Mr James, but Professor Jack failed to take it up. I would not hesitate to say that much of the 'problem' of rural transport has arisen from a crude and unsophisticated costing technique, that is only now, tragically late in the day, beginning to be superseded. The irony is that the small firms never practised it, yet always had a far better knowledge of their relevant costs than the big firms' managers had of theirs.

The Jack Committee also left me with a healthy suspicion of those who claim to speak for the ordinary people of Britain. I found it impossible to communicate with the representative of the Women's Institutes, whose picture of country bus services was quite unrelated to my own. More recently, I have heard sincere and high-minded representatives of consumers' organisations seeking to speak for bus users, and I have been unable to reconcile their concept of the problem with what I have seen. What people want in the country is access to certain benefits of the town: lower prices in the shops, professional services such as pharmacy, the law and local government, and the once-in-a-while opportunity to select 'consumer durables', such as fridge-freezers, fan-heaters and full-drop curtains, that make life significantly easier and more pleasant. If it is argued — as it well may be — that inter-active TV sales will make it unnecessary to go to the town for this, I still believe that country people (and townspeople too) will want the enjoyment of communal travel, and perhaps the visual, three-dimensional evidence of the quality of the goods they are buying. And, so long as there are the poorer as well as the wealthier, there will be the price-cutting of perishable goods that goes on at the end of the day on the market stalls.

Perhaps the Jack Report, which appeared in 1961, had the misfortune to be overshadowed by the appointment of Dr Beeching to mastermind the belated but inevitable trauma that brought the railway establishment 'kicking and screaming' into the era of the post-railway age. Just as the territorial bus companies held on to rural bus routes for whose provision they now seem to have

Two Crosville Bristols share the forecourt at Welshpool station. That on the right (an MW6G) is providing the service that ended passenger trains on the Welshpool & Llanfair light railway (now preserved); the other is an LH6P

A Bedford YRQ stops at the former Abbeydore station in the Golden Valley, on a journey from Hereford

been quite unsuited, so the railways in the 1950s went on providing services for which buses would have better adapted. The experience of the York to Scarborough line, which we looked at in chapter four, should have been the writing on the wall, but it was ignored for far too long, and the impact of railway closures, when it came, was too sudden for serious or sensible planning.

When the Eastern Region closed the former Midland & Great Northern lines through north Norfolk, before the Beeching closures were thought of, the Eastern Counties Omnibus Company contracted to replace them with a most expansive system of bus services, for which the region paid a subvention to cover the bus company's 'losses' — I use parentheses to indicate my reservations about the method of costing. These services attracted so little traffic that before long they were discontinued, as has happened to a great many rail replacement services since then. No one who had access to the figures could have doubted the necessity for rail closure, but no one who had any knowledge of the closure procedure could have been happy at how it was done, and the opportunity that was given for transferring traffic to rural bus services was almost everywhere thrown away.

The M & GN closures illustrate one aspect of this tragic story of mismanagement and inter-modal jealousy. Tediously long stage carriage routes, served by remarkably unattractive buses, were no proper replacement for the railway.

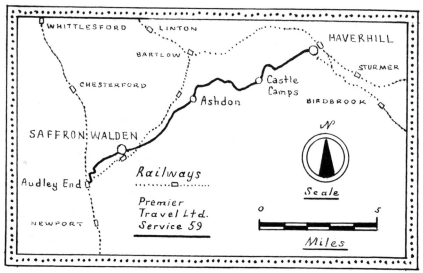

The logical way of replacing the Bartlow–Audley End railway, so as to keep the Haverhill–London traffic, and provide a new facility at Castle Camps

Yet limited stop semi-coach services connecting the principal traffic points might have kept the traffic, and provided connections with the remaining train services. Instead it was seen fit to design the bus services so as to connect each minor station and halt, so that they were a barrier to communication because of their slowness — comfort entirely apart. Yet where a profit-minded operator insisted on designing a replacement service to meet demand, considerable success could be achieved — a glance at the map will show how Premier Travel replaced the Bartlow–Audley End railway in Essex with a more direct bus service from Haverhill, that actually attracted new traffic, and minimised the subvention that was needed. (In the face of great opposition, the bus company even obtained — as a concession — a through season-ticket facility from road to rail!)

It is sad to think how much traffic was lost to public transport through the ineptitude of management in the 1960s, and the criticism must be shared between both railwaymen and those responsible in the supposedly 'associated' bus companies. In very few cases were the small private firms given a chance to replace a train service, but the co-ordination that was supposed to follow from railway investment in the territorial bus companies entirely failed to develop. Writing at the time, David St John Thomas in *The Rural Transport Problem* analysed the ineptitude of railway management and the failure of co-ordination, and all that I would add here is my own observation of the way in which railway management proved capable of retiming a train without notifying the bus company that had replaced the branch line service with which it connected — and then blaming the bus company because its timetable revisions came on a different date! Thus did bureaucracy rob the countryside of public transport — is it any wonder that car ownership is greatest in the rural counties?

Not that the railway managers were the only ones to display crass insensitivity in the days when bus traffic was already beginning to be lost to the car. In the same book we find the following example of how not to treat local councils when they are trying to help bus operators — the Totnes Rural District Council had sponsored a meeting of several councils with bus and railway officials.

> At the start, the bus spokesman said that he would like to emphasise that his attendance was experimental and did not create a precedent — an announcement which hardly warmed the air. Then, the council sought to have a particular bus timed five minutes earlier to enable passengers to catch a train. Without in any way commenting on the proposal or agreeing to consider it, the bus company replied that if the council 'objected' to the timetable, the proper course was to do so through the Traffic Commissioners.

It is fair to say that by no means every small operator was anxious to enter into discussion with the local council, and certainly the present generation of managers in the larger firms have rather broader horizons, but the great fall in bus traffic that has marked the past twenty-five years is in no small measure to be blamed upon the industry itself, which for so long displayed a false belief that it had a 'captive market'.

Through all these years the country bus services continued, tending to shrink but surviving against the odds. Vehicles that were out of date in the towns lingered on in the villages, much to the delight of the enthusiasts, and though no replacement appeared for the Vista, the small firms managed to keep their services going. The development of the minibus was thought by some to be the answer to the problem, but the trouble is that a service likely to be financially viable must carry about thirty passengers or so on some at least of its journeys, which means that a minibus would need to be duplicated from time to time, at considerable cost in wages. It is more economical to run a larger bus all the time, since the wage cost will be just the same as it would be for a minibus. (The best

The ultimate rural problem – 'no chimneys'. On an afternoon in 1971 a Bedford VAS of Evans of Penrhyncoch returns empty after working the Aberystwyth–Salem service

use of the minibus is now beginning to appear as the provision of high-frequency services in towns and cities, where traffic has in the past twenty years been increasingly driven away by operators running larger buses at less and less frequent intervals.)

The prosperity of the country bus in the decade after 1950 was undermined by a number of changes in rural society that were plain enough to be seen at the time, even though they were not always remarked upon. First there was the end of rationing, which meant that more money could be spent on food and clothes; petrol too became freely available for those who owned cars. Then the spread of mains electricity to rural areas brought with it the television set as an alternative to the picture house in the nearest town, and it is not too much to say that the wiring of each village meant the end of its 'picture bus'. The spread of car ownership, which began in the the early 1950s and continued with ever-increasing speed for the next thirty years, had mixed effects in the villages, but none of them was beneficial for the bus.

As early as 1956 the first signs of private car competition became apparent to those who were nearest to the market. One of our Corona services started from the village of Little Yeldham, running into Sudbury and back — just the two journeys — on a Thursday afternoon for the market. Every Thursday there would be half a dozen ladies waiting at the road junction by the church, where the bus turned round, and a few more at the Faggot & Stone at the hamlet of

Northend. After that the bus provided the only service Chapel Hill ever saw, before acting as a relief to the Gestingthorpe service from Belchamp Walter on. I recall this occasion because I was in the habit of conducting those journeys, and got to know the passengers; one sunny afternoon we pulled up at Yeldham and there was only one passenger. I asked, as she got on, where were the others? 'Oh, Mrs So-and-so came along and gave them a lift,' was the answer. 'She hadn't room for me.' Needless to say they were all waiting at a quarter to five for the bus home, and they all bought single tickets, but I hadn't the heart to say anything.

For there lies part of the problem (and what some say should be the solution). Country people help each other, and who would leave anyone they knew standing? (Still more on a wet day.) Gradually the traffic slips away, and there is no doubt that the car is a preferable alternative, especially when you can afford your own. And cars rapidly became common in the country, so that by the late 1960s the county with the highest number of cars per person was Radnorshire (and the lowest was Lanarkshire). Then, as agricultural workers came to need cars to reach the fields, and at the same time began to work shorter hours, the breadwinner's car became available for Saturday shopping. In many places the planners compounded the problem by removing buses from their traditional stands and making them use out-of-the-way bus stations, often using the former stands for a car park (Sudbury is a classic example of this).

The Mountain Goat has become part of the Lake District tradition, filling the gaps where larger firms with larger buses have had to withdraw. Here 'Little Billy' arrives at Glenridding from Ambleside, one day in 1978, when there weren't many Bedford OBs still in service

The country bus, like the country carrier, had one great attraction. It was there when you wanted it. When the shopping was done you could make your way to the bus — not too far away — and settle into your seat for a gossip until it was time for it to go. Just as the car began to be an alternative, the buses were moved on, and the larger firms, seeking more miles from each bus, tended to re-schedule services so that they no longer waited on the stand. Instead the passengers waited, come rain or shine, till it suited the bus to come and pick them up.

At the same time that alternatives to the bus were becoming available the social structure of the countryside was changing at unprecedented speed. Population statistics fail to show the nature of this change, for despite the shift of labour from the farms to industry, usually in the towns, there was a growing movement of middle-class residents into the villages. Here the private car played a big part, whether for those who bought cottages for retirement or for those whose work involved the need for independent transport. Neither of these groups generated demand for bus services to replace passengers lost as the old way of life began to disappear. Today the process has been carried so far, especially with the growing number of weekend residences, that in some

Another systematic exercise in providing rural transport. This Trent Bristol LH6L, photographed near Earl Sterndale in August 1981, is working a 'Peak Pathfinder' Sunday service between Ilam and Buxton, sponsored by public authority to improve access to the countryside

villages even the post office has closed, and there is virtually no local community at all, let alone a bus service. (The publicity given to the 'second home' problem by Welsh extremists should not blind us to its equally serious impact on some of the villages of Norfolk, to give but one example.)

Yet despite all this, the country bus is still to be found, and by no means always does it require heavy subsidy from the public purse. In 1968 the state acquired the last of the pre-war bus combines, that of the British Electric Traction Company, and the National Bus Company was formed (along with the Scottish Bus Group) to own and manage the territorial bus firms. In the 1970s the NBC found it necessary to withdraw from much of its 'deep rural' operation, and the county councils, which had been given transport co-ordinating powers in 1972, were happy to arrange for private firms to take over. In some counties the co-ordinating officers were able to play a useful part in suggesting new developments, and helping small firms to improve their publicity, while the counties were also given authority to provide subsidy, as the Jack Report had suggested more than ten years before.

Public subsidy has been criticised for 'throwing money at the problem', and indeed there can be few operators (there are some) who will say no to cash from the public purse. By far the greatest part of the subsidy so far provided has gone to state-owned companies, leaving many of the small country bus firms to carry on with reduced services, making the best of it.[1] Country bus operation, after all, has always been a matter of 'fine tuning', and we have seen that the local proprietor is usually better placed than the town-based manager to adjust to local demand. I have no intention to open the contentious subject of cross-subsidisation here — the supposed practice of 'robbing Peter to pay Paul' that has been claimed to be essential by the territorial bus companies — beyond pointing out that the reservations I have already expressed about costing apply also to this part of the business. It is sufficient here to record the financial skill of 'unlettered' busmen (and women too) who have succeeded in keeping services going through a period of increasing difficulty.

Several attempts have been made to relieve the rural transport problem, in which government, the large bus companies, and the Post Office have all been concerned. In Switzerland the Post and Telephone Organisation is the primary provider of rural bus services, and their losses have for many years been offset by the profits on the urban telephone service. It was often asked why the British Post Office could not combine the carriage of mails and passengers, and it must be accepted that no very satisfactory answer was ever given. In the 1930s it was not unknown for buses on late evening runs to carry letterboxes, chained to the vehicle, but these were mainly to be found on inter-urban services,

---

1 Out of £691 million subsidy to the bus industry in 1982–3, £499 million went to predominantly urban operators; £173 million to the state-owned companies, with much urban mileage; and only £19 million to private operators, mainly for rural services (White Paper, *Buses*, Cmnd 9300).

convenient as they must have been for the villages along the main roads they served. In the north of Scotland, too, there were examples of operators — David MacBrayne being the largest and best known — that had contracts for the carriage of the mails on specially adapted dual-purpose vehicles. But it was the conversion of the Post Office from a Department of State to a publicly owned corporation in the late 1960s that made all the difference.

As a corporation, the Post Office found that it could obtain investment allowances, and it began to use them to buy dual-purpose vehicles of its own. Some of these were Land Rovers, while others were converted Ford Transits and similar types of minibus. With these it was possible to offer accommodation for passengers on country rounds, provided they did not mind a slow and roundabout journey, calling at out-of-the-way farms and letterboxes. This contribution to the solution of the rural transport problem has been most extensive in Scotland, but there are services at various places throughout England and Wales — even in the Home Counties there are many inaccessible villages, and a postbus may be as valuable in Sussex as it is in Caithness.

The past twenty years have also seen the development of community transport, both in urban and rural areas, designed to encourage self-help and to make use of voluntary effort. Despite considerable drafting problems, because of the pressure of operators and trade unions to see that genuine businesses did not lose traffic, governments adjusted the legal framework of the bus industry to encourage this, and here and there, perhaps with the support of the local territorial company, community bus services have been established with some success. The law has also been changed to permit minibuses to be operated by charitable organisations with a minimum of control — a measure that is open to criticism in that the safety regulations that apply to commercial operation have been waived. Third-party insurance requirements for private cars have also been amended, to allow lift-giving that involves payment of out-of-pocket expenses — all in the hope that country people can be encouraged to help themselves.

In 1968 the government at last provided means for the payment of subsidy to loss-making bus and ferry services, and in 1972 the rearrangement of local government gave specific powers and duties to the non-metropolitan county councils (often called the 'shire' councils) to co-ordinate public transport in their areas. They were required to appoint transport co-ordinating officers to do it, and the idea seems to have been modelled on the work of the late Horace England, of the Devon County Council, starting some five years before. The operators, too — including British Rail — were required to co-operate with the council and with each other, and to provide information for the co-ordinating officer to use.

The effectiveness of this bureaucratic solution varied considerably from county to county, for political reasons, but the rural problem remained in the public mind. The Department of Transport then conducted various experiments — called RUTEX — which produced a certain amount of information,

Public authority is also responsible for the development of Community Bus Services such as this one at Halesworth, in Suffolk

but little further enlightenment. 'Experimental areas' were provided for, within which experiments could be made by county councils, but the procedure was hedged about with so many complications that it had little effect. Then in 1980 the government invited county councils to set up 'trial areas', within which the control of buses would be limited to the need for an operator's licence (required everywhere), which covers mechanical efficiency, financial standing, 'good be-haviour', and professional competence. Firms holding such a licence were to be able to provide services without the need for a route licence as well.

There were three applications for trial areas — in mid-Norfolk, mid-Devon, and the former county of Herefordshire. In the first two the consequences were hardly significant (showing perhaps that the route licensing system was already a dead letter in the deep rural areas), while the Hereford scheme became a *cause célèbre*. The trouble was that few generalisations could be made from it. There was a period of rapid competition and change in the city, but that was an isolated case, whose relevance to the rest of the country must remain doubtful, while the main effect on the country bus services was to tighten the control of them by the Hereford and Worcester County Council, through its system of subsidies that is not always matched in other parts of the country.

As this book is being written, the government is putting through parliament its plans to free the bus industry of route licensing over the whole country out-side London. Many prophets of gloom are to be heard. While for my part, I do

At the end of the lane, the bus still serves the village. A Crosville Bristol LH6L passing through Llanfihangel-y-Creuddyn on the Pontrhydfendigaid–Aberystwyth service in the summer of 1982

not expect the apocalypse, neither do I see the Bill as providing the solution to the rural transport problem, for, as we have seen, its causes lie deep within the nature of rural society. I do expect to hear a lot of ill-informed comment, from people — in and out of the House of Lords — who purport to speak for the countryman.

The rural transport problem has not been reduced since David St John Thomas published his book in 1963, but it has changed. The country railway is now a rarity, though what an opportunity has been thrown away for its continued usefulness by unimaginative bureaucracy and absurdly expensive standards on the part of railway engineers! The big bus companies are still in the business, and since a new generation of managers has come to the fore, I detect a greater understanding of the problem, and a more sophisticated approach to costing, so that I am not unhopeful. The survival of the smaller business has been remarkable, and although there are those who fear the impact of the present government's legislation upon them, I do not altogether share those fears. I recall the nature of country bus operation as we have seen it, in which a living can be made from a variety of functions, and while there may be no fortunes to be made, there is by the same token the less likelihood of severe competition.

What worries me most is the threat of overmuch subsidy, not just of the country bus, but of the country way of life. To throw money at the problem is a form of pauperisation, and the strength of the country bus has always been its assured place in a local community that needed it, and was prepared to pay for its services. A healthy profit and loss account is a cause of self-respect, and of that independence that the countryman prefers to feel. When all is said, I for one am not happy about country bus services being provided by people who see the country through urban eyes. In this book I have tried to evoke the buses of past days; even the older ones that the horses drew, and the carriers that linked the villages of yesterday. I have tried to show what it has been like to work on the buses, or to manage the country bus firm, and to bring out the associations between the buses and the people they serve. For the country bus belongs to the countryman, to an extent that was never true even of the country railway — there is no superior officer 'up the line'. That has always been its strength, and long may it so remain.

12 Out On The Road

What was it like to work on the country bus — what is it like still? In this final chapter you are invited to come out 'on the back' — the busman's traditional term for the conductor's job. This is not an attempt to recreate an actual conducting duty, but more of a composite picture of the country bus of the late 1950s as I knew it in the Essex and Suffolk villages served by what local people referred to as 'the Corona'.

It is ten past eight on a sunny morning, and most of the fleet is already out. While our driver backs CCF 595, a Leyland Tiger, out of the running shed, we go into the office across the road to collect the bag and punch. The brown leather cash bag has a float of 10s (50p) in change, and the ticket machine is in a square black metal box. Slinging the bag over the shoulder, and signing for the float, we pick up the box and cross back to the yard. The only other essential items of equipment, which we already have, are the T-shaped 'budget key' for opening and closing the boot, and the conductor's badge which the law requires us to wear — this has a sort of half-moon attachment at the back, intended to go through a buttonhole, but we slip it into a slot cut into the strap of the cash bag.

The bus is ready now, the driver up in the cab gives us a wave, and we climb in. A couple of raps on the bulkhead and he is away, while we sit on the front seat inside the door and open the ticket box. Inside there is a machine with a handle at the side, which fits on to a plate attached to a shoulder strap; it has a slot for tickets to go into, and there is a ticket rack with packs of singles, returns and parcels tickets. (These are all we shall want, but if we were working the London service there would be others, such as day-returns and exchange tickets.) The shoulder strap goes on so as to cover the strap of the cash bag, as a protection against the rather unlikely event of someone — possibly a drunk — trying to get at the money, but we don't fit the machine on to it yet.

The duty board.says 'Dead to Great Maplestead to take up Service 29', so we settle down to enter the opening numbers on the waybill, from the counters on the machine and the ticket packs on the rack. There are some people already waiting for the 8.35am from Lavenham, which provides a commuter link from three or four villages to Sudbury, but we go by a more direct road, and soon we have passed through the town and are climbing the long Ballingdon Hill up into Essex. On the way we meet a 29-seat Vista in our colours, one-man operated, working the 8.15am from Halstead. He has about twenty passengers, which is a good load.

At Maplestead there are two people waiting. We open the door as the coach pulls up, and they climb in with a word of thanks — the service has only recently been extended to the Maplesteads, and we don't know many people yet. It is the same at Little Maplestead, but now there are four people on board it is worth going round for the fares, so we fasten the ticket machine to its plate. Three returns and a single, and so far no ten shilling note to reduce the change in the bag. There is a request for the time of the bus back, and then we return to the front, to stand and look ahead at the road.

Leaving the Maplesteads, which are tidy villages, with big trees and hedges, we cross a bit of 'prairie', where the hedges have been grubbed out and the fields stretch across the landscape with few breaks — not so extensive as they are further north in Suffolk, but bleak, and liable to produce drifts of snow across the sunken roads in the winter. It is a relief when we turn and drop down to the beginning of Gestingthorpe at Box Iron Corner, called 'Seven Sisters' on the timetable. (It takes its familiar name from the triangle of green where the three roads meet, reputed to resemble the old-fashioned irons into which the house-wife had to put hot coals from the range.) There are three or four people here, all familiar, and our first pushchair, which means getting down and going round to the boot.

Now we stop several times as we go up the street. (Not that it is like a street in a town — there are no pavements, and cottages and farms alternate with fields.) It's a fine morning, and we can leave the door open while we go round for the fares, leaving the driver to stop when he sees a passenger, and signalling him to start with a couple of rings on the bell. (We need to know just where the bell-pushes are, because they are mounted on the underside of the luggage rack, and are not easy to spot when you are standing up.) At the Stores there is an old man who needs helping up the steep steps, so we break off the collection of fares to go back to the door, and then we're on our way to the last stop in the village, at Foundry Corner: two more pushchairs and a small folding pram, leaving us not much room in the boot.

Now we dip down to a brook, and climb up again, through more hedgeless fields, to the tiny village of Belchamp Walter (local people tend to call it Walter Belchamp — there are also Otten and St Pauls Belchamp — which makes it sound like something from *The Archers*). Here there are four or five passengers waiting, all elderly, all of them old friends, so we stay for a chat when we take their fares. The next few miles are along empty lanes, with 'no chimneys' as the busman's jargon has it, till we turn uphill again to the village of Borley.

Borley is famous for its ghost, and there may be a comment from someone about whether we ought to stop for it; there is not much point, though, for our one regular passenger is not waiting on the green today. We are high above the Stour valley here, with the clear East Anglian sky over-arching us, and the view is one to savour — even though we've got fewer than twenty passengers in our 35-seater. At the bottom of the hill we pick up one more, the crossing-keeper at the Rodbridge railway gates — and then we turn on to the main road, and run down into Sudbury. Since no one will join us now we can make up the waybill with the 'finishing numbers' for the journey (making sure we've entered the service number and journey time at the head of the column), and put it away, with the ticket machine, in the box on the rack.

As we pull on to the stand, we slide the door open and slip down before the coach comes to a stop. It's mildly dangerous, but very commonly done — a sort of demonstration of the skill of the trade, I suppose. We go round and open the boot, and then come back to the door to help people down, and there are smiles all round, and 'See you later, then', and 'Will you be on the bus when we go back?' Two of the Maplestead passengers have found they are related to a couple from Belchamp, but the other two seem a bit stand-offish, as if the bus was a bit beneath their dignity. Perhaps Maplestead is like that . . .

It's a quarter to ten, and the London coaches are already on the other side of the road — one of our passengers from Gestingthorpe is going to go on to Romford. At 9.50am the service coach — the Regal III 33-seater — leaves with a full load, and the Vista that has come through from Bury St Edmunds follows, to work relief to Chelmsford, where it will turn and relieve the 9am from London back again. Some of its passengers will have come in on the Halstead bus we met on Ballingdon Hill, earlier on, for the London coach service is also a local bus at the country end of the route.

We're not on again till the 11am circular, so the driver parks 595 on the forecourt and goes off in search of a coffee. This gives us time to check over the

Hold on .... I'm sure I've got some string in 'ere somewhere!

charts for tomorrow's excursions, and see if there will be enough seats on the London service, given the present state of the bookings. One of the evening journeys up to London looks tight, and there's nothing to be made by cancelling an excursion now, because the 38-seater is well loaded for Brighton (at a guinea (£1.05) a time — it has the right sound for the Brighton fare), and Clacton is going to run as well. So we'd better ring Miss Beeston and see if her brother will turn out and cover Hadleigh to London, returning light. That done, we pencil in some plans for tomorrow's orders, and it's time to go out again.

This time we do a circle, taking back some of the people we brought in and picking up others. Back in time to see the down service from London through at twelve o'clock, pick up a bit of lunch in a café, and off again to cover the 1.15pm from Maplestead. In the course of the lunch break, we decide not to run another relief coach on the Clacton excursion: there are 60 booked so far, and we've allocated a 41-seater and a 29, but we could always use a 35-seater and put the 29 on to the evening tour, which does not make so much money. So we instruct the clerk to ring the agents in the villages, and record any bookings they may have made since they last notified us. They must then be told to stop booking, for we shall be able to sell the remaining seats at the office. Two full loads on Clacton won't make a lot of money at 5s (25p) a time, and two-thirds for children, but they are regular customers, and it's good to know we shall have no empty seats, because at that fare you can't afford them.

Two more trips round the Essex villages in the afternoon, with full shopping bags as well as pushchairs in the boot, still leave us time to slip into the back office and type out the daily orders for Sunday. Finally we are back in time to provide a relief to the 2pm from London, which comes through Sudbury at five o'clock. On Saturdays there will be the passengers who have come into the town for shopping; more local traffic joins the coach than there are London passengers getting off, and a relief is scheduled as far as Lavenham. So three of our vehicles set off down the Melford Road: the Regal III, back from London, the 29-seater that will work through to Bury St Edmunds, and ourselves. The London driver takes the daily orders, which he will pin up in the old garage at Acton, because we shall have more stops to make on the way. As a result we both reach Lavenham together, where we wave him off down Water Street while we turn 595 round, and park it outside Mr Fisk's greengrocery shop (which is also our booking agency). After we've seen the driver back into the side road and draw out again we go in for a chat about the Clacton bookings — Mr Fisk is sorry to have had to turn three late bookings away, but he understands the reason, for he too is trading on narrow margins, and selling a perishable product.

Now our driver is waiting, and we have a habit of visiting the back bar at the Swan for two halves of bitter and a game of darts in the half an hour before we go back to Sudbury with the picture bus. The ticket machine goes back in its box, but we keep the strap on to hold the cash bag in place. Playing darts with a cash bag — by now quite heavy — on your shoulder is quite an art, so we probably shan't win! The two halves reflect the need to be sensible about our drinks, and also the requirement of etiquette that the driver buys his round, and doesn't have to accept a pint from the guv'nor without making his own contribution. In fact there is little time before we must get back to the bus for the 6.15pm to Sudbury.

The greengrocer's shop is closed now, but several passengers are already in their seats, for these will be younger people who find no difficulty in sliding open the door. By the time we've stopped at the housing estate on the edge of the village we have more than half a load, and the rest we make up when we stop at our own village of Acton. They all get off at Sudbury at 6.40pm, and we have two hours off for our tea.

Three more trips, and the day's work is done. The 8.50pm to Lavenham and the 9.20pm back again are hardly worth running (though since the driver will have to be paid for his time anyway, there's not a lot of cost involved). At 10.30pm the last buses all leave — ours for Lavenham and Monk's Eleigh, one for the Gestingthorpe circular and one for Long Melford and Glemsford; another one for Cavendish left at 10.15pm. Dusk has fallen as engines start up, and the buses pull away, taking home the people who came in to the pictures, those who have been in the pubs, and some who have been spending an evening with friends. When they have all gone the streets will be empty, and silence will descend on the town.

We have a standing load, though, which means squeezing among people in the aisle of the bus to get the fares in. We take the direct lane to Acton, which is still narrow, with high banks in places; there is a blueish haze over the landscape. Good-nights are exchanged as people leave the bus at the depot, and we continue through lonely roads to Lavenham, setting down a crowd at the housing estate. After Lavenham there are very few left on the bus, and conversation has died now — we all sit and keep our own company. All but one have left at the end of Brent Eleigh Street, and we can make up the waybill for the last time. Then at Monk's Eleigh we help the driver reverse at the foot of the green, in one of the least known of Suffolk's lovely villages, and set off for home, with the interior lights turned off, in gathering darkness. I think there is something very special about those last few miles, when 'the horses begin to smell the stable', and the day's work is almost done.

But not quite. Half an hour before midnight, and the depot is still busy. We are the last of the picture buses to come in — there is still a belated coach party somewhere on the road, and the 11.15pm will have not long left the coach station at King's Cross — but lights are on in the yard and the running shed as we pull up by the pumps. Rules are firm — every vehicle must be filled up, and the oil checked, before it is put away, and while the driver is seeing to this, we've got to sweep out. Then the coach will be ready for whatever needs arise in the morning. To start with, we empty the ashtrays.

It's not a very nice job, even though they slide out to let us tip the contents on to the floor. If dog-ends and ash are all we find, we shall be lucky, for when you get apple cores and toffee papers you have a mess on your hands. And best be on the look out — it's not so long since one of us found a broken up razor-blade in the mess in an ashtray. While we do it, we throw any rubbish we find on the seats to the floor, and then take a quick look along the luggage racks for any lost property. (We remembered to check the boot when the last pushchair was taken out, on the five o'clock relief.)

Now we can fetch a broom, and sweep everything to the front of the bus, where our driver, his chores completed, holds a box against the steps to catch it. While we empty that into the big rubbish bin, CCF 595 is driven over to the running shed, and the engine is shut down for the last time today. Silence reigns, apart from a few good-nights, and the sound of cars being started and driven away home. We have still to put the ticket machine away in the office, and lock up, though — and there's the day's takings to be cashed up and balanced with the waybill; that can be left till we get home, and we'll pay in tomorrow.

It's been a good day. We've met old friends, watched the sky change, commented on the promise of harvest. All our passengers are home now, with something gained from what we have provided. The sound of a diesel still rings in our ears, long after the engine has shuddered to silence, and the twisting lanes come back to our vision as we close our eyes. This is not a job you can do without being involved in it. Conductors on town buses have just to hurry about, trying to get all their fares in, and never seeing the passengers as individual people — so much the worse for them. There are few modes of transport that, like the country bus, form an integrated part of the community that they serve, and that's the satisfaction of it.

Bibliography and Acknowledgements

By way of thanks, I would like to dedicate this book to all those whom I got to know, whether staff or passengers, when I was in the country bus business myself, with Premier Travel of Cambridge from 1948 to 1952, and again ('on the back', as a part-time conductor) in 1955–6; and with Corona Coaches (and subsequently with Jack Mulley) from 1956 to 1960. To them must be added a host of names of people who have shared my enthusiasm for both the countryside and its buses — one name must stand for them all, which is that of Eric Axten, who has contributed the maps for this book.

As David St John Thomas said of *The Country Railway,* the book has been fun to write, for it has taken me back to many other works that sit on my shelves, waiting to be re-read, only mostly there is never time. To David, therefore, special thanks are due, for commissioning the book, and then for taking an interest in every chapter and suggesting improvements, most of which I have been more than happy to accept (for those I haven't, the liability is my own!) I am grateful, too, for his foreword. I am also most grateful for all who have helped me to find illustrations, and above all to my colleague, Jim Bray, who has done the drawings.

Another of the pleasures of making the book has been the interest and encouragement of many friends, among whom I would like to record thanks to Richard Storey, of the Modern Records Centre at the University of Warwick, and to John Hickman and Peter Redwood, fellow members with me of Carrs Lane United Reformed Church, Birmingham.

This book makes no pretext to scholarship, so an exhaustive bibliography is uncalled for, but in addition to listing the principal items I have made use of, I include some titles that readers may like to go on to, if I have whetted their appetite for more. I hope I shall offend no one by sins of omission, for there is a large, and largely arcane, literature on the subject of buses. Reference has been made to the standard work, W. T. Jackman: *The Development of Transportation in Modern England* (2nd Edn, 1962). This monumental study ends before the development of the motor bus.

I tried to give the outline history of the industry in *The History of British Bus Services* (1968), and to add a bit more detail in parts of *The Bus & Coach Industry* (1975). There is an immense quarry of data in my old friend, the late Charles Klapper's *Golden Age of Buses* (1978), drawn from his encyclopaedic knowledge of the industry. Very useful material is to be found in R. J. Crawley, D. R. MacGregor & F. D. Simpson: *The Years Between* (Vol. 1, n.d., Vol. 2, 1984, Vol. 3 awaited), a detailed study of the National Omnibus & Transport Company and its successors. Other important texts include J. Cummings: *Railway*

Motor Buses and Bus Services in the British Isles, 1902–1933 (1978); David Holding: *History of British Bus Services — The North East* (1979); and Colin Morris: *History of British Bus Services — South East England* (1980). One book that gives continued pleasure is Keith Turns: *The Independent Bus* (1974), which provides as a series of case studies numerous illustrations of the subject-matter found here.

On the serious problems of rural transport, David St John Thomas has written a book that is by no means out of date: *The Rural Transport Problem* (1963). More recently we have had M. J. Moseley: *Accessibility: The Rural Challenge* (1979), which was preceded by the report on the research upon which it was based, M. J. Moseley, R. G. Harman, O. B. Coles & M. B. Spencer: *Rural Transport and Accessibility* (1977), in two volumes. The Rural District Councils Association published a pamphlet which is a full report of a conference on the subject: *Rural Transport: What Future Now?* (1971) — reading it today one sees how little the world has changed.

Pamphlets on the subject, varying in general interest, are abundant, and I will restrict myself to a few that should have an appeal beyond the magic circle of bus enthusiasts! Eric Axten: *A History of Public Transport in the Halstead Area* (1980) provides a continuous analysis of all forms of transport within a specific district, and gives both breadth and insight beyond the local interest. Two pamphlets by D. E. Brewster: *Motor Buses in East Anglia 1901–1931* (1974) and *Motor Buses in Wales* (1976) provide abundant illustrations of our theme. Finally, I have made use of Philip Lingard: *First Bus in Yorkshire* (1975) for its fascinating study of the story of Ezra Laycock's business from start to finish.

Any writer on the industry must acknowledge his debt to the Omnibus Society, the senior enthusiast organisation which is so much more than just that. Out of many publications — and this is to pass over the back numbers of the *Omnibus Magazine,* which are a fruitful source — I would mention C. J. Davis: *Travelling Hopefully* (1982), which describes various journeys by country bus, and three monographs by J. E. Dunabin: *Wye Valley* (n.d.), *Hereford Transport* (1970), and *Yeomans of Canon Pyon* (1978). (If any reader wants to join the Omnibus Society, then write to the Honorary Secretary at 6 Ardentinny, Grosvenor Road, St Albans, Herts, AL1 3BZ.)

For part of the background I have drawn on the books of the late S. L. Bensusan, which so far as I know are today all of them out of print. For a foreigner, he did a wonderful job in picturing the people of God's own county, before the industrialisation of agriculture and the spread of commuting turned Essex into just one of the Home Counties, not much different to the despised 'sheers'. If there is nostalgia in this book — and how should there not be — it is for the loss of a way of life that went back a thousand years. Throughout that time, country people travelled to market, and sought entertainment, and in due course the motor bus came along to help them to do so.

Index

Numbers in *italic* refer to illustrations